Y
w
Ple
C

REMAINING A CATHOLIC
AFTER THE MURPHY REPORT

This work is dedicated to my brother Aiden Egan (1949-2010)
who died during the writing of the book

Kevin Egan

Remaining a Catholic
after the Murphy Report

the columba press

First published in 2011 by
the columba press
55A Spruce Avenue, Stillorgan Industrial Park,
Blackrock, Co Dublin

Cover by Bill Bolger
Origination by The Columba Press
Printed in Ireland by
Brunswick Press Ltd, Dublin
ISBN 978 1 85607 740 8

Contents

Introduction

I can vividly recall the days following the publication of the Murphy Report. We had been given advance notice to prepare for some shocking revelations. As with other shock-provoking events, nothing prepares one for the event when it arrives. Like many Catholics I couldn't claim to be a disinterested observer. This was my church they were talking about – not just the Catholic church worldwide, but the Irish Catholic church and the diocese in which I now reside. I had lived in Dublin for most of the 70s. Could all this have been going on under my eyes and I was blind to it? Of course the answer is yes. Child sexual abuse takes place behind closed doors, it is surrounded with secrecy and kept hidden from the public view. In those days people did not disclose incidents of abuse to the authorities, and when they did, it often failed to enter the public forum.

Following the publication of the report, I found myself having to come to terms with a number of disturbing truths: the extent and horrific nature of the abuse; the institutional cover-up on the part of church authorities; my assumption that church leaders could be relied upon to do the right thing, especially when it concerned vulnerable children. I listened to politicians, health care professionals, church leaders and media commentators give their responses to the report. Most especially I was interested in the reactions of ordinary people. This led me to pay more attention to the letters to the editor section of the newspapers than I normally would. In the week following the report I facilitated a conversation among students and staff at the place where I work, All Hallows College. As I listened to expressions of shock, betrayal and anger, it became clear to me that Catholics needed a space where they could converse about these matters that concerned them. While some might avail of opportunities provided by their parish, there were many for whom this would not be their environment of choice.

I discussed with colleagues ways in which an educational in-stitution like All Hallows College might facilitate such a convers-ation. I decided to offer a short six-hour module called: *Remaining a Catholic After the Murphy Report*. It would be part of the Renewal for Ministry Programme and open to participants in the programme as well as those coming from outside. Over forty signed up. The group included clergy, religious and laity. All had connections to the church but at different levels. Some described themselves as 'just hanging on by a thread.' (A de-tailed breakdown of the composition of the group is provided in the appendix). As the weeks went by they expressed apprecia-tion at having a place where their views and experiences were accepted. While the scandal impacted differently on group members I could see common ground emerging around the factors that contributed to the emergence of the scandal and the reforms that were necessary if the church was to regain some credibility.

As I listened to the views of the lay people in the group, I found myself moving towards the view that if one were to de-cide to remain in the church it could only be on condition that one would be allowed to function within it as an adult. Things could not go on as before and the subservience of the past could have no future. It was as if the experience of listening to sur-vivors had woken up the laity to finding their own voice. They had seen survivors come forth with the courage to tell their story and demand that they be listened to and have injustices addressed. If one part of the church could begin to relate to lead-ership in a different way, then maybe the other parts of the church could do so as well.

As I did the research for the module, I thought of presenting the material to a wider audience. I first thought of writing an ar-ticle for publication but soon realised that an article could not do justice to the topic. It would require a book. I explored the possi-bility of sharing the workload and co-authoring the book with someone else, but abandoned the idea when I realised that this would involve the same amount of work, if not more.

As I retrace my steps I can see that I did not set out with the intention of writing a book on this topic. Rather the book emerged from other ventures I had undertaken.

As I went about writing the book I became concerned about how the book would be perceived by the reader. Would the book be seen as an attack on the church or as defending the institutional church? As I gave some thought to this question I realised that the book, if it is to achieve balance, could equally be seen from either perspective. If all the readers of the book were to see it fulfilling just one function, then I would have failed to present the material in a balanced way. I further came to realise that in my own mind I had been equating a balanced stance with an objective stance, and they are not the same. I don't claim to write from a purely objective stance. I write as someone brought up in the Catholic tradition and the subject matter of the book has personal relevance for me. On the other hand, as a health care professional and college lecturer, I bring both clinical and research training to the undertaking which allows me to write with a certain level of objectivity. Ultimately it is the prerogative of the reader to make the final judgement as to the balanced treatment of the subject matter.

One of the first questions a publisher asks when presented with a manuscript asks: is who are you writing this book for? When asked the question I have stated that I am writing this book for 'critical' Catholics. The word critical allows me to move away from the categories of practising and lapsed. It refers to people who, either in this present moment or at some time in the past, have made their spiritual home in the Catholic church; who have some affinity with its tradition and spirituality. When the credibility of that church has been undermined as a result of the clergy sexual abuse scandal, they have a natural desire to understand the nature of the crisis and what contributed to it. For some of these people the crisis will give rise to questions of belonging. Do I want to continue belonging in this church? If I do, what changes or reforms do I want to see? Questions such as these are hinted at in the title I have given to the book: *Remaining a Catholic after the Murphy Report*.

I am assuming that the reader of this book has questions he/she wants answered. These are many and varied. If I were to narrow them down to three, I would say they are: What in fact happened? Why did it happen? Where do we go from here? Chapters one to three address the first question, chapters four to seven explore the second question and chapters eight to ten take up the final question. A feature of the book is the series of questions for reflection and conversation which conclude each chapter. I have several reasons for including this feature. I hope that it will add a conversational tone to the book, in the sense that the conversations with the reader continues after the chapter has ended. My intention is that it will provide an opportunity for the reader to reflect on some of the material presented in the chapter. One of my hopes for this book is that it might be read and discussed by groups of people. These could be members of a book club or a spirituality group or parish group who might make use of the book to facilitate their own discussion of the topics presented. I expect that some of the questions will have more relevance than others, depending on the interests and concerns of the reader. I expect that the reader will choose for themselves whatever questions have relevance for them.

The term Catholic features in the title of the book and I have chosen to make this the topic of my first chapter. I have done this with some reservations: it might discourage some readers from buying the book or it might lead them to skip the first chapter. Reactions such as the ones I have described are sometimes due to the fact that many people are of the opinion that there is only one way of being Catholic. Charles Taylor, a Canadian scholar on religion, wisely observed that where 'Vatican rule-makers and secular ideologies unite is in not being able to see that there are more ways of being a Catholic Christian than either have yet imagined' (2007, 504). If the Vatican persists in defining Catholicism in narrow and confining terms, then more and more Catholics will no longer describe themselves in this way. The Catholics I am writing this book for are a broad parish of believers, ranging from those who are fully signed up members to those who would describe themselves as 'critical Catholics', and those who may have been brought up in the tradition but now see themselves as having no spiritual home while continuing to pursue a spiritual quest. They might be described as 'spiritual Catholics' since their spiritual roots are there. They include some who could be described as pre-Vatican II Catholics (born before 1941), others who might fit the description of Vatican II Catholics (born 1941-1960), and finally a much younger group who might be referred to under the broad title of post-Vatican II Catholics (born after 1961). (D'Antonio *et al*, 2007) This latter group would have less exposure to Catholic teaching than the other groups, less institutional commitment, and less involvement in the life of the church. It goes without saying that the reaction of each of these groups to the material presented in this book will be different.

CHAPTER ONE

Catholic in One Way or Another

The crisis in the Catholic church arising out of the clerical sexual abuse scandal has been making media headlines for the past fifteen years in Ireland. I followed the unfolding crisis, not from the stance of a disinterested observer, because it was my church they were talking about. As the story unfolded I found myself distancing from that church while at the same time remaining connected to it. I was exposed to new shocking truths about the church and how it functioned. I found myself moving from a childhood stance of idealisation to an adult stance of disillusionment. I find it helpful to think of this as a continuum consisting of two end points with various degrees in-between. This helps explain the title I have chosen for this chapter: Catholic in One Way or Another.

In this chapter I am going to invite you to think about two words: Catholic and Identity. I will first treat of them separately and later attempt to co-relate both terms. I will begin with the term identity since everyone functions out of some sort of identity. At the outset let me draw a distinction between personal and collective identities. Personal identity refers to characteristics that are unique to the individual, for example someone may be considered friendly or distant. Collective identities include those that are socially ascribed: for example, race and gender. They also include membership of groups with whom we identify e.g. footballer, musician (Templeton & Eccles 2006, 252). All of us have multiple collective identities and personal identities out of which we function. In terms of these collective identities I could describe myself as a white, male, Catholic, psychotherapist. The terms Catholic and psychotherapist could function as either a collective identity referring to a group I identify with, or they could function as a personal identity describing who I am. My sense of who I am could be said to be made up of both my personal and collective identities. Spiritual identity could be considered as part of one's personality identity, whereas religious identity refers to the religious group one belongs to and would be considered as part of one's collective identity (Templeton & Eccles 2006, 253).

Identity is Multidimensional
Identity can also be said to be made up of the following three components: a cognitive component, for example beliefs; an affective component, for example values, and a behavioural component, for example attendance at a religious ritual. Combining all these together I could describe myself as a Catholic, who believes in Christ's presence in the Eucharist, who values belonging to a community and who regularly attends Mass.

When one considers Catholic identity, the question can be asked as to whether this is an assigned collective identity or a chosen collective identity? A young person growing up in a practising Catholic family is likely to develop a Catholic identity by reason of the socialisation process operating within the family. Such an identity is closer to an assigned collective identity than a chosen collective identity. Later on in young adulthood, the same person may go through a crisis of belief upon the resolution of which he/she may make a conscious choice to embrace their assigned Catholic identity and so move closer to the chosen end of the continuum (Templeton & Eccles 2006, 253). The present clergy sexual abuse crisis might lead that same person to another crisis whereby he/she decides to revisit that earlier decision.

A recent book edited by John Littleton and Eamon Maher, *What Being A Catholic Means to Me* (2009) tells the story of several Catholics who decided to do just that. One of the contributors, Conor Brady describes himself as a 'Cradle Catholic'. For him Catholicism would seem to be both an assigned and a chosen identity: 'I have been given my Catholic faith as my gift. I embrace it as such – I know I am fortunate' (2009, 89). Another contributor, Colm O'Gorman makes a different choice. Colm has written about being sexually abused as a child by Fr Sean Fortune. As a result of this traumatic experience he finds himself in a position where he 'could not possibly belong to this church which at an institutional level so betrayed me and the values it professed' (2009, 160). While he did not formally leave the church he just came to realise that he was no longer part of it. Being Catholic could no longer be part of his collective chosen identity.

Before going any further, I feel I need to give some consideration to the term Catholic. It comes from combining two Greek terms, *kata* and *holos*. The literal translation of the words would be 'including everyone to work together'. This implies bonding together as a community in which all are welcome (Groome 2002, 244). The term was first used by St Ignatius of Antioch (circa 107) in his *Letter to the Smyrnaeans* (McBrien 1994, 3). Later the term was incorporated into the Nicene Creed at the Council of Constantinople in 381 along with the other marks of the church: one, holy and apostolic. The American theologian Richard P. McBrien makes the point that as an adjective, the term Catholic is a qualification of Christian, just as Christian is a qualification of religious, and religious is a qualification of human. In other words, to be Catholic 'is to be a kind of human being, a kind of religious person and a kind of Christian' (1996, 4). He emphasises that Catholicism is first of all a way of being human. However important Catholicism might be to one's identity, it is important to acknowledge that it is not a primary identity category.

What Kind of Catholic Am I?

I expect the initial reactions of most readers to this question would be to think of themselves in terms of being a 'good' Catholic or a 'bad' Catholic. Those who think of themselves as 'bad Catholics' are usually those who consider themselves as 'bad' since they don't live up to the moral teachings of their church. In the words of James Carroll: 'Bad Catholics were in bad marriages, or they were openly gay, or they had abortions, or they practised artificial birth control' (James Carroll 2009, 288). Since there was an identifiable group of bad Catholics this permitted the other group of good Catholics to feel morally superior since they considered themselves to be in good heterosexual marriages, were opposed to abortion and either abstained from sex or practised natural family planning methods. In the light of the clerical sexual abuse scandal one could ask the question: who are the bad Catholics now? (James Carroll 2009, 290). Whatever validity lay behind such a distinction has now been shattered to pieces. In fact, there was never any validity to the distinction since all Catholics are sinners and for that reason every Eucharist begins with a ritual of repentance.

Having discounted the moral undertones of this question, I will now explore it from a more objective stance by looking at the different ways of being Catholic. Sociologists of religion distinguish between different ways of being Catholic. Dean R. Hoge proposes the term 'Parish Catholic' to describe those for whom Catholic identity is important and central. As the term indicates they are involved in parish life, frequent the sacraments and accept the institutional authority of the church. He distinguishes between these and a group he calls 'Spiritual Catholics'. For these their Catholic identity is important but they do not take an active part in parish life. They would describe themselves as committed to some of the Catholic teachings, spirituality and traditions, but not to the institutional church (Hoge *et al* 2001, 181). Finally, he uses the term 'Contingent Catholics' to refer to a group of people for whom their Catholic identity is 'contingent' on other identities such as the family or ethnic group they belong to. They are neither church-going Catholics nor spiritual Catholics, yet they see themselves as Catholic and expect to remain so (Hoge *et al* 2001, 181). The existence of this group serves to illustrate how Catholicism, like all other forms of religion, is not just a system of beliefs but a cultural phenomenon. It is contextual. It exists at a particular time and in a particular place. For this reason we can speak of Irish Catholicism as a distinct entity. It is different from English or French Catholicism. An Irish Catholic integrates two collective identities, being Irish and being Catholic. This illustrates how identity is multidimensional. Religious identity, ethnic identity and family identity are all interrelated.

The collective identities I speak about here are not static. They are dynamic. This is true both on a personal and a collective level. As I go through the life cycle, my religious identity changes. It is open to both internal and external influences. For example, following the Second Vatican Council, for many

Catholics, Catholic identity took on new dimensions (Dillon 1999, 25). When I was growing up as a child in Leitrim my Catholic identity had an anti-Protestant quality to it. The theology of Vatican II, along with personal and professional contacts with a wide spectrum of Christians from other denominations, challenged my childhood assumptions and helped change my understanding of what it meant to be a Catholic Christian.

Spiritual or Religious
One of the emerging trends today is that more and more people readily make a distinction between being religious and being spiritual. Having a collective religious identity is one possible pathway to a spiritual identity (Templeton & Eccles 2006, 254). Many of those people referred to in the category 'Spiritual Catholics' would describe themselves as spiritual but not religious, or they might describe themselves as both. In research conducted by Zinnbauer *et al* (1997) almost 40% of those interviewed agreed with the view that spirituality is a broader concept than religiousness. They were also of the opinion that while being religious and spiritual overlap, they are not the same concept. The Canadian spiritual writer Ronald Rolheiser, in his best selling book *The Holy Longing*, gives a graphic illustration of the relationship between the two concepts. He contends that we are all spiritual whether we see ourselves as religious or not. For him spirituality 'is more about whether or not we can sleep at night than about whether or not we go to church' (1997, 7). Just as we are human before we are Catholic, we are spiritual before we are religious. Being spiritual is at the core of what it means to be human. As Rolheiser would say, spirituality helps us deal with the existential issues of life, such as fear and anxiety – the things that keep us awake at night. Spirituality is not incompatible with religion. For a great majority of people it was their collective religious identity that gave rise to their spiritual identity.

It may come as a surprise to you to know that many atheists consider themselves to be spiritual (Andre Comte-Sponville 2007). Because they don't consider themselves to be religious doesn't mean they don't see themselves as spiritual. According to them, the human spirit is universal. People readily confuse religion with spirituality and therefore dismiss spirituality. It is this same 'categorical error' that leads them to conclude that athiests can't be spiritual. Religion could be described as the institutional side of spirituality. It consists in the system of beliefs, rituals and teachings that characterise a group of religious people. Spirituality, on the other hand, is more inner directed, less visible and more subjective. It is more existential than creedal (Tacey 2004, 8). Spiritual writers identify three components of spirituality: connection, compassion and service. When we feel connected to something larger than ourselves we are usually moved to make a contribution to others and to the world (O'Hanlon 2006, 71).

When it comes to finding out whether people consider themselves spiritual or religious, researchers ask them to choose one of the following statements:

- I am spiritual and religious
- I am spiritual but not religious
- I am religious but not spiritual
- I am neither religious nor spiritual

How would you choose to describe yourself? In research conducted among American Protestants by Marler & Hadaway the majority of respondents saw themselves as both religious and spiritual (64%). However, when they reviewed the findings comparing successive age cohorts they found that the younger cohort were less likely to see themselves as religious and spiritual, slightly more likely to see themselves as spiritual only, and much more likely to see themselves as neither (2002, 298).

I believe that the personal impact of the clerical sexual abuse crisis is determined by a number of variables. For Catholics one of these is their level of identification with the church; whether they are Parish Catholics, Spiritual Catholics or Contingent Catholics. Likewise, those who consider themselves to be religious, religious and spiritual, or just spiritual will have different levels of attachment to the church institution and are likely to experience the impact of the crisis differently. It is readily acknowledged by all commentators that the present crisis is causing distress to all Catholics, especially those closest to the church. While the proportion of Catholics in Ireland who could be described as 'Parish Catholics' is estimated to be lower than

60% (Dowling 2000, 51) there remains a large proportion of people who fit the description of Spiritual or Contingent Catholics.

I hope to explore in the following chapter how the crisis is experienced by this wide and varied group of people. Teresa Dowling, a sociologist at UCD, has remarked that in a society in which it is almost natural to be Catholic, it is virtually impossible to escape the influence of Catholicism (2000, 55). Since this is so, it is virtually impossible for people living in Ireland not to have been impacted by this crisis in one way or another.

A Catholic Crisis

We normally associate the term crisis with an event of limited duration. The tsunami crisis in East Asia in 2003 is one such example. The first public acknowledgment of the clerical sexual abuse crisis by Pope John Paul II was in June 1993 in a letter written to the American Bishops (Doyle 2007, 154). This crisis has not been of short term duration. It has gathered momentum since then and is still very much with us. Fr James Martin SJ has called it the 'greatest and gravest crisis in the history of the Catholic Church in the United States.' (2007, 139). Fr Hans Küng has described it as the 'worst credibility crisis since the Reformation.' (The Tablet, 24/04/2010). At this early stage in the book I am not going to make a judgement as to the nature and severity of the crisis. However, it is appropriate that I should say something about the nature of the crisis. If I were to put it in the form of a question, I could ask what was at the core of this crisis? Was it the abuse of minors by individual bishops, priests and religious or was it the manner in which these allegations and those making them were treated by church leadership? To opt for the latter does not imply that one is discounting the former but it does convey that the roots of the crisis go much deeper than the instances of sexual abuse in themselves. Bishop Howard J. Hubbard of the Diocese of Albany, New York, showed an appreciation of this when he described the scandal as 'two-fold'. 'There is the two-fold scandal of the breach of sacred trust by individual priests and the way bishops like myself have mishandled such misconduct, because of ignorance, fear or the misguided attempt to protect the church from scandal.' (2003, 60).

This is one of the most open acknowledgments of the nature of the crisis/scandal by a church leader that I have come across.

The full realisation of the extent and depth of the crisis has been slow to dawn. It is only now, after a period of seventeen years since the UTV *Suffer Little Children* programme about Fr Brendan Smyth was first broadcast in 1994 that we are in a position to realise the full extent of this crisis. It was in 2002 that the BBC broadcast the Panorama programme *Suing the Pope* and we had the RTÉ Prime Time special *Cardinal Secrets*, both of which highlighted the manner in which church authorities dealt with allegations of child sexual abuse by clergy. Arising out of these programmes we had the Ferns Report published in 2005 and the recent Murphy Report in 2009. Sections of the Report which were withheld from publication then were published in December 2010. The Murphy Commission of Investigation into the Diocese of Cloyne has submitted its report to the Minister for Justice and we are awaiting publication.

For Reflection and Conversation:
What kind of Catholic are you: parish, spiritual or contingent?
Do you consider yourself to be spiritual or religious or both?
What is your view that there are different ways of being Catholic?
Can you identify the moment when you became aware of the full extent of the clerical sexual abuse crisis?
Would you agree with Hans Küng's assessment that the church is facing 'the worst credibility crisis since the Reformation'? If so, why?

CHAPTER TWO

The Impact of the Sexual Abuse Scandal

In the previous chapter I made reference to the distinction between Parish Catholics, Spiritual Catholics and Contingent
Catholics. It is important to keep this distinction in mind as we
explore the impact of the clergy sexual abuse crisis on the faithful. The closer one is to the church the greater the impact of the
scandal. This also applies to the manner in which one goes about
interpreting the scandal. Non-practising Catholics will be less
likely to distinguish between Catholicism itself and the bishops
as its leaders, so they will readily condemn both together.
Predictably the crisis has evoked a wide range of responses. On
the one hand you have those who desire to see the elimination of
all vestiges of Catholicism from Irish society. On the other, you
have groups similar to the Voice of the Faithful (VOTF) in the
United States calling for a radical reform of the church. Finally,
there are others locked in denial who still claim that the crisis is
largely the creation of the media. As an example of those who
seek the elimination of all vestiges of Catholicism, I quote from
an article by the *Sunday Independent* columnist Emer O'Kelly
who said she would 'welcome the destruction of all the Catholic
Church in Ireland stood for, including the culture which used
helpless children as labourers and objects of sexual fulfilment'
(*Sunday Independent*, 6/12/2009). Interestingly enough, those
seeking reform in the church also desire the elimination of the
culture which contributed to the abuse and its cover-up.

Emer O'Kelly raised the question of whether churches have a
contribution to make to society. I am of the opinion that they do.
There is a sizeable number of people, who might not describe
themselves as card-carrying Catholics, yet they would like to see
vibrant churches contributing to the wellbeing of society and to
what we today call social capital. Fintan O'Toole, a columnist
writing in *The Irish Times*, expressed sadness at the potential loss

of Catholic church influence following the Murphy report: 'The world into whose coffin the Murphy report has driven so many nails, the world in which Catholic beliefs and institutions play so central a part, is too imaginatively rich to be dispensed without deep regret' (*Irish Times*, 5/12/2009). One can get a sense of what O'Toole is referring to by reading John McGahern's essay *The Church and Its Spire* (1993). There he expresses a sense of gratitude for the 'spiritual remnants' of his Catholic upbringing. This is the 'Catholic religious sensibility' that sociologist Andrew Greeley speaks of (Greeley 2004, 102). For McGahern it includes 'an awareness of mystery and wonderment, grace and sacrament, and the absolute equality of all women and men underneath the sun of heaven'. He is prepared to acknowledge that these 'remnants' remain even though he no longer believes: 'That is all that now remains. Belief, as such, has long gone.' ('The Church and Its Spire' in *Love of the World: Essays by John McGahern* 2009, 133).

Do I Stay or Do I Leave?

For many adult Catholics the question of leaving or staying in the church never arises. Yet, following the publication of the Ferns, Ryan and Murphy reports* this question has become a live issue. There is a website aptly named *Count Me Out* which provides a facility for those who wish to formally leave the church. As of February 2010 more than 7, 000 people had used this website to formally leave the church. The journalist David Quinn expressed surprise that the figure was not higher given the current mood and the publicity the site has received (*The Tablet*, 27/02/2010). The Archdiocese of Dublin has recently issued a statement from the Vatican saying that the sacrament of baptism precludes 'opting out' officially because theologically the sacrament can't be revoked. The archdiocese has plans to provide a facility for those who wish to formally register their intention to leave (*The Irish Times*, 16/10/2010). The news

---

* In 2005 the Ferns Report was published. It investigated the handling of clerical child sexual abuse allegations in the diocese of Ferns. In 2009 the Commission of Investigation into Child Abuse (Ryan Commission) published its report into the abuse of children in residential institutions and industrial schools.

agency Reuters reported that a quarter of German Catholics were considering leaving the church in the wake of revelations of clergy sexual abuse there. The situation in Germany is somewhat different than in Ireland. There, citizens are to register as a member of a church so that a percentage of their taxes may be passed on to that church. The decision to leave the church may simply be a protest move to withdraw from this scheme.

Just as there are those who are drawn to the church by inner promptings and by what they observe externally, there are those who are drawn to leave by the same inner promptings and what they observe externally. There are those who for deep personal reasons feel that they can no longer remain inside the church and they either privately or publicly leave. On 23 February 2010, Bernice Donoghue, a survivor of clergy sexual abuse, wrote an open letter in *The Irish Times* to Archbishop Martin stating her wish to be 'excommunicated' from the church. I would describe her writing this letter as an act of self differentiation. 'I do not want to be a member of a church that aided and abetted a paedophile so that he could rape and sexually abuse me for four years of my childhood.' (*Irish Times*, 23/02/2010). She was abused by the Norbertine priest Brendan Smyth. In the letter she outlined six reasons why she does not want to be a member of the institutional church. I expect that many Catholics like me on reading the letter wondered whether they too wanted to be a member of such an institution. For those of us who decide to stay we do so conscious of the fact that we are members of a flawed and dysfunctional institution. We do so with a sense of shame for what has happened in our name. The Augustinian priest/poet Pádraig J. Daly found the words to describe this shame:

> We huddle in our upper room,
> The doors bolted,
> For shame at our betrayal
> Of all that is tender
> (*In the Light of 'Ryan' Afterlife*, 2010, 62).

One could not but be impressed by the clear and dignified manner in which Bernice Donoghue expressed her desire to no longer belong to the church. The need to separate oneself from the institution which gave credibility and protection to the abuser is one felt by many survivors of clergy sexual abuse. The Australian Bishop Geoffrey Robinson tells how in his pastoral care of survivors he has on occasion found himself helping a victim who grew up Catholic to find a path in life outside the church (Robinson 2007, 219). In his view, respect for the dignity of the victim and their journey towards wholeness may demand such a pastoral response.

Those Who Stay

Contrary to media reports, many baptised Catholics do not display a tendency to leave the institution, though their relationship with the church may change during the course of their life. In a study of spirituality among American baby boomers, Wade Clark Roof (1993) found that 81% of those who grew up Catholic still identified themselves as Catholics in adulthood. Mainline Protestants had a retention rate of 65% and conservative Protestants had a rate of 80% (Dillon 1999, 7). In an effort to explain why Catholics tend to stay in the church, Andrew Greeley points to what he calls 'Catholic religious sensibility'. By this he means a collection of metaphors and stories which attempt to explain what human life is all about (Greeley 2004, 102). According to Greeley, approximately half of those who leave the church do so because of marriage to someone who is not Catholic. Greeley notes that a high percentage of American Catholics, while dissenting from Catholic teaching on a number of ethical questions, notably divorce and contraception, will continue to be active members of the church. What holds them there is 'the intensity of their religious imagination, experience and imagery.' (Greeley 2004, 76). This is another way of saying that they find a spiritual home in the church. It is important to keep this in mind as we explore why Catholics continue to stay in the church following the clergy sexual abuse scandal.

While the Murphy Report and others had a profound impact on Irish Catholics, one should not underestimate the holding power of the Catholic imagination and spirituality on those referred to by Breda O'Brien as 'ordinary decent Catholics (ODCs) (*The Irish Times*, 24/04/2010). Their reasons for remaining in the church are many and varied. In a recent *Would You Believe* programme on RTÉ, Mick Peelo asked one of the participants, who described herself as a survivor of clerical sexual abuse, if she would consider leaving the church. The starkness and simplicity of her reply still rings in my ears: 'Where else would I go?' I suspect that there are many like her who simply don't wish to leave the church for the very reason that it is their spiritual home. However, the decision to remain in the church can still be problematic for Catholics. 'By remaining,' asks Oliver Maloney, 'are we facilitating the survival of a model of church which regards itself as unaccountable?' (2010, 8). This is a valid question. Since the publication of the Murphy Report life can not go on as before. One cannot go on being a Catholic in the old way.

Forms of Distancing
When there is conflict or anxiety in a marital relationship, family therapists draw attention to the emergence of forms of distancing that occur between the partners in the relationship (Gilbert 1993). In marriage, divorce is an extreme form of distancing. Likewise, for Catholics, leaving the church could be described as an extreme form of distancing. However, there are other less obvious forms of distancing which take place. I suspect that many of us have engaged in one or other of these following the publication of the Murphy Report. I believe that over the past few years Catholics have engaged in some of these behaviours either consciously or unconsciously:

- Abandonment/decrease in religious practice
- Withholding financial support
- Reluctance to engage in prayer
- Keeping one's distance from church leaders, e.g. local clergy
- Increase in levels of criticism
- Emotional withdrawal
- Considering leaving the church

Just as in a relationship, such distancing behaviours are likely to precede a more extreme form of distancing such as leaving the church. When one notices these behaviour patterns one is then faced with a choice of either continuing with the distancing or re-engaging in some way.

How Do You View the Crisis?

We have been looking at the impact the clergy abuse scandal has on our sense of belonging in the church. It is possible to describe this crisis as existing on a variety of levels:

- a crisis of faith
- a crisis of credibility
- a crisis of leadership
- a crisis of belonging
- a crisis of loss

I asked this question of participants in a course I taught at All Hallows College in April/May 2010. (For a detailed account of the questionnaire responses see Appendix). The majority of respondents (53.7%) viewed it as a crisis of credibility, with 24.4% seeing it as a crisis of loss and 9.8% viewing it as a crisis of faith. This response confirms the assessment made by Vincent Travers OP: 'It is not so much a crisis of faith as a crisis of credibility and without question a massive crisis of credibility for the young.' (*Religious Life Review*, April 2010, 133). The journalist David Quinn describes it as one of confidence in the institution of the church and in the leadership. He thinks that the more general crisis of faith can be attributed to factors such as secularism while the crisis of credibility/confidence can be attributed to the scandals (*The Tablet*, 27/02/2010, 9). Since I agree with this view, I will be exploring the crisis in terms of credibility and loss rather than in terms of faith and belief.

The terms crisis of credibility and crisis of leadership are interrelated since it was episcopal mismanagement and poor leadership that lead to the loss of credibility. The crisis of credibility has also contributed to the crisis of belonging. It diminished people's trust in the church and its ministers. This in turn weakened their sense of belonging and their emotional connection with others in the church (Dokecki 2006, 210). In my view, a crisis of credibility is the most accurate way to describe the impact of the clergy abuse scandal. However, this does not deny that the scandal does have a profound impact on faith. This impact is not so pronounced when one considers faith in terms of belief. People still continue to believe in God and in Jesus Christ.

However when one looks at faith in terms of trust (the affective dimension of faith) then the crisis undoubtedly has had a profound impact on one's faith.

The priest/psychologist Stephen Rossetti insightfully observes that the crisis poses a tension for the believer as he/she attempts to reconcile two conflicting realities: i) some priests and religious have sexually abused children and the institutional church has not always responded appropriately and ii) priests and the institutional church are symbols of the divine. According to Rossetti, there are three possible ways in which one can try to resolve this tension. One can attempt to deny the reality of the sexual abuse allegations; one can decide to leave the church; or one can move to a higher or more sophisticated level of faith – one which can embrace contradiction and paradox. Using Fowler's model of faith development, Rossetti talks about a transition to a post-conventional stage of faith development (Rossetti 1996, 98). This possibility of a resolution to one's faith crisis is also alluded to by the former vice-chairman of the Northern Ireland Policing Board, Denis Bradley. He views the crisis as challenging 'all of us to embrace the deep spirituality and the mature faith that is a strong aspect of our inheritance' (*Doctrine & Life*, Vol 60, No 6, July/August 2010, 3). He believes that as people of faith we have the resources to meet this challenge in our rich spiritual heritage. For such people the church means more than the people who run it.

Crisis of Credibility

A brother of mine, recently deceased, when he wanted to describe someone whom he respected would say: 'I have great time for that person.' He was referring to credibility. It is what makes a human relationship viable and it applies not just in the interpersonal realm but to the political, economic and religious areas of life. In this context it refers both to individuals and institutions. Credibility is a major issue for churches who seek to have influence over their members and in the wider society. For the people of Jesus' day he was seen as a credible leader. They saw him as someone 'who taught them with authority' (Mt 7:29). His credibility was not institutionally conferred, in the sense that he wasn't an official teacher (rabbi) in the Jewish religion, though the people gave him that title (Mk 5: 35). His authority seemed to have come from a coherence between what he said and what he did. Whether it is a case of an individual or an institution, once a gap appears between what one proclaims and how one behaves then credibility is undermined. Marie Collins, a survivor of clergy sexual abuse, describes her experience of this gap: 'I could not reconcile the church I thought I knew all my life with the church I was now seeing up close' (in Maher & Littleton eds, 2010, 60). Marie Collins is not alone. Survivors of abuse and Catholic faithful readily speak about this loss of credibility. This loss is more pronounced among the younger generation and among those whom I described in chapter one as 'Contingent Catholics'. For some, the loss of credibility has led to understandable cynicism (Garry O'Sullivan, 2010, 149). It would add further to the crisis if church leaders were to underestimate the extent of this loss of credibility.

For many brought up in the Catholic tradition, the credibility of the church was something bestowed from on high. It goes back to Jesus' words to Peter: 'on this rock I will build my church' (Mt 16: 18). It was passed on to Peter's successor, who today is Pope Benedict XVI. This theological understanding of credibility needs to be complemented by a sociological understanding. Here credibility comes from the bottom up; it is a gift from the members of an organisation to the leadership. Applying this to a church context one can say that the 'authority of any religious denomination or local church is a 'gift' from the lay believers to the faith community, not an inherent possession of leaders or something given to the community by them. It is grounded on a transaction of normative trust' (Anson Shupe, 2007, 104). I will be basing my analysis of the clergy sexual abuse crisis on this understanding of credibility.

Internal versus External Credibility
In today's world, church leaders need to take on board this understanding of credibility. They also need to come to terms with the broad population with which churches need to maintain credibility. It includes two groups of people: the 'internal community' made up of believers and supporters and equally important, the 'external community' of society at large. There is a

perception that under the leadership of Pope Benedict XVI there is a tendency to give priority to the internal community; to speak to the faith remnant and to distance from the secular world. If this perception is accurate, this approach would represent a serious missed opportunity. 'In the long run, an 'authentic' religious community must maintain some enduring balance with both' (Shupe, 2007). If one is to acknowledge the impact of the crisis on church credibility one has to be aware of the impact on both groups, the internal and the external community. The credibility of a church leader doesn't just depend on his standing with the internal community.

A *Sunday Tribune* survey which examined the credibility of institutions in Irish society underlines the extent of the loss of credibility. In 2001, 6% of the sample reported losing trust in the Catholic church, in 2010 the figure had risen to 32%. The corresponding figure for banks was 41% and for government 44% (21/03/2010). It is clear that the church is not the only institution in Irish society with a credibility problem. Like any other social institution, it should be concerned about loss of credibility. The political philosopher, Onora O'Neill has observed that trust 'is hard earned and easily dissipated. It is an invaluable social capital and not to be squandered' (2002, 7). The Catholic church is a worldwide institution and its credibility will vary from country to country. In 2008 a survey conducted by CARA in the United States found that eight out of ten American Catholics described themselves as 'somewhat' or 'very' satisfied with the leadership of Pope Benedict XVI and more than seven out of ten were at least 'somewhat' satisfied with the leadership of the American Bishops (John Allen 2009, 422). I will return to this issue of credibility when I look at the levels of satisfaction expressed by Catholics with the bishops and Pope following their response to the Murphy Report.

A Crisis of Loss
When it comes to exploring the impact of the crisis, one needs to distinguish between the impact on primary victims, i.e. those who were the victims of clergy sexual abuse, the secondary victims, i.e. members of parish congregations in which the abuse occurred, and tertiary victims, namely society at large. (Shupe,

2007, 122). This is especially true when it comes to exploring the crisis in terms of the losses experienced by those different groups. Loss is a powerful metaphor with which to view the crisis. I have drawn up a list of the different groups who in one way or another have undergone loss. These include:

- the victims of abuse
- their families, friends and acquaintances
- the perpetrators and their families
- the faithful
- those in a leadership position in churches, bishops and religious superiors
- priests and religious
- society at large

In order to get a sense of how any of these groups experienced the crisis one just has to look at what each group lost as a result of the crisis. I begin with the victims of abuse. Their losses include:

- Loss of innocence (intrapsychic)
- Loss of control
- Loss of self-esteem
- Loss of dreams
- Loss of ideals
- Loss of bodily integrity
- Loss of trust (interpersonal)
- Spiritual loss
- Loss of faith

Some of these losses are psychological, some biological and some spiritual. Since the spiritual losses are not often acknowledged in the literature, I would like to focus on them. Bishop Geoffrey Robinson, whom I quoted at the beginning of this chapter, describes these losses well. He refers to sexual abuse by clergy as a form of spiritual abuse. He points out that 'in sexual abuse there is always spiritual harm, for abuse always harms the person's sense of wholeness and connectedness and hence the person's sense of meaning and identity' (Robinson 2007, 231). In chapter one we saw that spirituality has to do with connection, meaning and identity. Marie Collins, whom many in Ireland

have come to admire for her role in exposing the crime of child sexual abuse by clergy, describes her experience of spiritual loss: 'I am sad to lose an important part of my life. My family and I had always been involved in our parish. My son had been an altar boy, my husband a member of the choir and I a member of parish groups. I ask myself can I ever find my way back' (Collins, 2010, 60). Her words convey vividly how the abuse scandal, as well as being a crisis of loss, is also a crisis of belonging.

The secondary victims of clerical abuse have been the ordinary decent Catholics (ODCs) who placed their faith in an institution that betrayed their trust. For many, their sense of loss is linked to a sense of shame because they identified so closely with the institution. A few years back I attended a concert featuring among others Eleanor McEvoy. That night she sang a song called *Ave Maria* and introduced it by saying that she wrote it out of a feeling of empathy for her mother whose faith, which was a source of consolation, had been taken away from her. In the song she appeals to Mary not to let her mother down even if the institution she placed her faith in had. I quote a verse from the song which poignantly conveys her heartfelt prayer:

Ave Maria, don't let her down
In your powder blue robe and your shiny
gold crown
See, she put all her trust in you
Like she was brought up to do
So Ave Maria don't let her down
You can't let her down
(*Ave Maria*, Eleanor McEvoy from the album *Early Hours*)

The sense of spiritual loss experienced by faithful Catholics is something personal to each believer but it also has a corporate or group dimension. This was brought home to me as I read an article by a Catholic layperson, Ned Prendergast, in *The Furrow*. He referred to the picture we cherished of ourselves as 'the caring church of warm hearted people – with a heroic history of service'. This picture has been shattered, and with this shattering 'has disappeared part of our belief in ourselves' (Ned Prendergast, *The Furrow*, April 2010, 199). He is referring to the sense of pride which many of us had in being Catholic and being

Irish. That pride has been taken away. A cousin of mine recently told me a story of attending an Anglican church service in Swansea and introducing herself to the lady sitting next to her as an Irish Catholic. The lady curtly responded: 'Well, that's not something to be proud of, is it?'

The losses for priests and religious and those involved in church leadership (bishops) are many and varied. First, there is the loss of credibility I referred to earlier. The ministry of all these people depends on trust. When that trust is undermined so is the very core on which their ministry depends. Ministry is not easy at the best of times, it is all the more demanding when 'the precious values of trust and regard on which their minister-ial lives are founded have been eroded or lost' (Johanna Merry 2010, 23).

A Church Community in Grief

I have been drawing on the metaphor of loss to explore the nature of the sexual abuse crisis. A church experiencing loss is also a grieving church. Eamonn Conway, writing in *The Furrow* in 2002, described how the Catholic church in Ireland was in a state of grief and he illustrated this by naming some of the typical grief responses, shock, denial, anger and guilt. From today's perspec-tive, it would seem that the element of shock and denial has di-minished but the sense of anger and guilt continues. In order to get a sense of where we are today I find it helpful to draw on a model developed by William Worden. According to this model individuals and groups dealing with grief have to address the following four tasks:

• Accept the Reality of the Loss
• Process the Pain of Grief
• Adjust to a World Without the Deceased
• Find an Enduring Connection With the Deceased in the Midst of Embarking on a New Life (Worden 2009, 39-53)

Each of the groups I have identified, victims, leadership and faithful, are in their own way having to address these tasks. The term 'deceased' as used in the model could be taken to refer to life before the abuse took place or before it became public. Adjusting to a world without the deceased could mean letting go of one's previous assumptive world, for example, an idealistic view of the church, of priests and bishops. For some who decide to leave the church it would mean finding another spiritual home outside the institutional church. For those who stay, finding an enduring connection with the 'deceased' might mean holding on to some sense of Catholic identity in the midst of this crisis. For the abused this could mean holding on to some sense of self and maintaining a spiritual connection. For church leaders, the tasks of grieving involve acknowledging the reality of abuse, listening to the pain of victims, and adjusting to a world in which the protection of vulnerable children becomes a priority.

In this chapter I have set out to explore the impact of the clergy sexual abuse crisis. The scandal has posed many questions to the Catholic church both on a leadership and a membership level. For some, the question has been do I leave or do I stay? Leaving, as we have seen, is an extreme form of distancing which does not preclude other forms of distancing by those who choose to stay. We have also explored different dimensions of the crisis highlighting faith, credibility and loss. This leads us to name some of the tasks facing the church at all levels as it comes to terms with grief.

Questions for reflection and conversation:
What forms of distancing have you engaged in following the publication of the Murphy Report?
Did you consider leaving the church because of the clergy sexual abuse scandal?
Do you know anyone who has left the church because of the scandal?
How do you view the present crisis?
Do you view it primarily as a crisis of credibility or a crisis of loss?
What losses have you experienced as a result of this crisis?

CHAPTER THREE

Documenting the Crisis

I have decided to limit my review to a study of the Dublin/ Murphy Report and the documentation surrounding it. I do so for two reasons. This Report has generated more comment and analysis in Ireland than any other report. Secondly, the findings of the report repeat and elaborate on many of the observations of other reports – the Ferns Report (2005) and the findings of the Review Board set up by the American Bishops: 'A Report on the Crisis in the Catholic Church in the United States' (2004). What distinguishes the Murphy and the Ryan Reports is that they are commissioned by outside, governmental agencies. The Catholic church operates as a closed system. It is not surprising that it took an investigation by outside agencies to penetrate the secrets of this closed system. Richard Sipe, the renowned US commentator on the clerical abuse crisis has observed: 'The ecclesiastical structure crumbles or at least trembles when external examination or exposure penetrates it' (Sipe, 2007, xix). In Ireland we witnessed the 'trembling' of the structure in the months and weeks following the publication of the Murphy Report.

The Report is the work of a Commission of Investigation into the Catholic Archdiocese of Dublin set up by the Minister of Justice in 2006. Justice Yvonne Murphy was appointed its Chairperson. The Commission issued its report in July 2009, which is commonly referred to as the Murphy Report. A series of legal challenges delayed the publication of the report. On 19 November the High Court authorised the release of an edited version of the report and it was published on 26 November. Chapter 19 of the Report and sections of Chapter 4 dealing with the case of Fr Tony Walsh were not published because he was facing criminal charges. It was released for publication on 17 December 2010 following his conviction on charges of sexual abuse and his sentencing to 16 years in jail. In accordance with its terms of reference, the work of the Commission covered the period January 1975 to May 2004. It made the decision to examine a representative sample of complaints covering that period. It examined complaints in respect of over 320 children against 46 priests, 11 of whom were members of religious orders (I. 10). Of the 46 priests examined, 11 pleaded guilty to or were convicted in the criminal courts of sexual assault of children (1. 11). The majority of complaints involved males: 2.3 boys to every girl suffered abuse. This reflects the findings of worldwide studies, where the greater proportion of victims of clerical sexual abuse tends to be males.

Findings of the Report
The remit of the Commission was to examine how complaints of clerical sexual abuse of children were dealt with by the archdiocesan authorities. The key finding of the Report appears in Par 1. 36, where it states categorically that 'all the archbishops and many of the auxiliary bishops in the period covered by the Commission handled sexual abuse complaints badly.' Fr Pádraig McCarthy in an analysis of the 45 cases in which the Report gave an assessment, concluded that twenty-five cases received some sort of approval from the Commission in terms of how they were dealt with, while 20 cases received varying degrees of criticism (Pádraig McCarthy 2010, 72).

The Report makes shocking reading. Archbishop Martin is on record as to his personal upset on reading the revelations in files submitted to the Commission. The strength of the Report is the clear and clinical manner in which it states its findings. This is especially true when it comes to examining the reasons for the inadequate response on the part of diocesan authorities. I quote what I consider to be the central conclusion:

> The Dublin Archdiocese's pre-occupations in dealing with cases of child sexual abuse, at least until the mid 1990s, were the maintenance of secrecy, the avoidance of scandal, the protection of the reputation of the church, and the preservation of its assets. All other considerations, including the welfare of children and justice for victims, were subordinated to these priorities. (Par 1. 15).

The Commission's findings reinforce what many comment-ators have observed about the clergy abuse scandal. It consists of two scandals: the sexual abuse of children by clergy and the attempted cover-up by church authorities. The Report further suggests that the reasons for the cover-up are systemic in na-ture. It concludes that in some cases the cover-up led to the con-tinued abuse of children while the alleged perpetrators were al-lowed to continue in ministry. The significance of the Report goes beyond the clinical conclusions it arrived at. Of equal im-portance is the fact that it gave a voice to the voiceless and pro-vided a record of their suffering at the hands of perpetrators and church leaders.

The Case of Fr Tony Walsh
Several chapters of the Murphy Report are devoted to an indepth examination of how allegations concerning specific priests were handled. Publication of Chapter 19 of the Report was held up pending criminal proceedings against Tony Walsh, a former priest of the archdiocese. On 7 December 2010 he was sentenced for the sexual abuse of three children. In Chapter 19 of the report he is referred to as Fr Jovito. It describes him as 'probably the most notorious child sexual abuser to have come to the attention of the Commission (Par. 19.2). I have chosen to describe his case in some detail as it illustrates very well the failures identified by the Report in the handling of allegations on the part of the Archdiocese over the period 1975 to 2004.

Fr Walsh was born in 1954 and ordained in 1978. His first as-signment was to the parish of Ballyfermot. Two days after his appointment a complaint was received by the diocese that he had sexually abused an 8 year old boy (Par. 19.5). According to the notes of Monsignor Alex Stenson who, as Chancellor of the Archdiocese, was dealing with his case he admitted to abusing young boys at least once a fortnight during his eight years in Ballyfermot (Par. 19. 31). In February 1986 he was moved out of Ballyfermot and assigned to Westland Row parish. At the time the diocese knew he was a serial abuser and he himself had ad-mitted to the abuse of three children (Par. 19.24; 19.123). It is es-timated that at that time at least seven priests of the archdiocese were aware of his behaviour (Par. 19. 13). It is the considered view of the Murphy report that the reason behind this move was to avoid any further scandal in Ballyfermot (Par. 19.24).

Fr Walsh has admitted to abusing over 100 boys (Par. 19.74) and to abusing before he was ordained (Par. 19.3). In 1988, ten years after his ordination, he was removed from parish work and sent for treatment to Stroud in England (Par. 19.34). Dr Desmond Connell was appointed Archbishop in 1988; the Report gives him credit for acting decisively in this case once he became Archbishop (Par. 19.124). In January 1992 Cardinal Connell initiated canonical proceedings against him. In August 1993 the canonical court gave its verdict that Fr Walsh should be dismissed from the clerical state (Par 19.86). In October he appealed his case to Rome. He was partially successful in this. Instead of dismissal from the clerical state he was required to stay in a monastery for a period of ten years (Par. 19.89). Archbishop Connell wrote to the Roman Rota outlining his disappointment with this decision (Par. 19.98). He eventually petitioned Pope John Paul II to dismiss Fr Walsh and in January 1996 a decree was issued by Cardinal Ratzinger confirming the dismissal.

While Archbishop Connell is given credit for acting decisively, the case shows up the failure on the part of successive church leadership to deal with a known serial abuser and to respond to complaints dating from the time of his ordination. The Gardaí had concerns about Fr Walsh dating back to 1990 yet the diocese did not inform them of their concerns (Par. 19.127). Here we have a situation where the diocese considered Fr Walsh responsible for offences that warranted dismissal from the priesthood but did not consider it necessary to inform the civil authorities about the related criminal offences. An insight into the thinking of church administrators at the time can be gained from the reflections of Monsignor Sheehy, a leading canon lawyer in the archdiocese, who referred to the 'outrageous suggestion' of Auxilliary Bishop Eamonn Walsh that the civil authorities should be informed (Par. 19.52).

Irish Bishops' Response to the Murphy Report
To evaluate the response of the bishops as individuals and as a

group one needs to apply two criteria: i) what does the response acknowledge? and ii) how adequate is this as a response?

The first statement I present for consideration was issued by the Irish Bishops Conference on 9/12/2009.

> We are deeply shocked by the scale and depravity of abuse as described in the Report. We are shamed by the extent to which child sexual abuse was covered up in the Archdiocese of Dublin and recognise that this indicates a culture that was widespread in the church. The avoidance of scandal, the preservation of reputations of individuals and of the church, took precedence over the safety and welfare of children. This should never have happened and must never be allowed to happen again. We humbly ask forgiveness.

It is clear from reading this statement that the bishops accept the judgement of the Murphy Report (Par 1. 15) quoted above. They express their own shock and shame and acknowledge the inadequacy of the response to victims of abuse by their brother bishops in the Dublin Archdiocese. They acknowledge the attempt to cover-up the scandal and go further to admit that this was made possible by a culture of secrecy which sought to protect the public image of the church and the clergy. Furthermore, they resolve to take steps to ensure that this will not happen again. An impartial observer would have to acknowledge the forthright and comprehensive nature of this response. Later, when we compare it to the Pastoral Letter of Pope Benedict, we will see that it goes further in admitting the cover-up and the cultural/systemic factors that enabled it. Again, compared to the responses of individual bishops mentioned in the Murphy Report it is markedly less defensive, which is to be expected. It is interesting to compare this statement to the one coming from the Vatican two days later following the visit of Archbishop Martin and Cardinal Brady to Rome. The Vatican statement expresses distress and regret 'at the actions of some members of the clergy'. However, there is no mention of the inadequate response by church leaders to complaints nor to attempts at cover-up. The statement from the Vatican did announce that the Irish hierarchy would be invited to Rome to meet with Pope Benedict and discuss their response to the Murphy Report.

This meeting took place in the Vatican on 16/02/2010. The meeting was unprecedented and from the Vatican's point of view was a statement that it was taking the situation in Ireland very seriously. In the view of one commentator this event turned into a PR disaster (David Quinn, *The Tablet*, 27/02/2010). We live in a world where images speak louder than words. In the memorable words of Susan Sontag: 'To remember is more and more, not to recall a story but to be able to call up a picture' (2003, 80). The 'picture' that remained with people following The Six One News that evening was one of the Irish bishops in full attire bowing to kiss the Pope's ring. The message conveyed was one of deference, where the bishops went to Rome to get their knuckles rapped for letting down the Pope and the church. No doubt, important concerns such as the welfare of victims, failures of church governance and the inadequacies of canon law were also on the agenda, but these never got an airing in public. The meeting concluded with a promise of something more to come in the form of a Pastoral Letter from Pope Benedict to the Irish church.

The Pastoral Letter

If one is considering offering an apology and addressing concerns of victims and of the faithful, then a pastoral letter would seem to be a more appropriate vehicle than issuing press statements which had been the mode of communication up to now. To do justice to the pastoral letter it is important to read it more than once.

The pastoral letter was expected to arrive during the Lenten season, and in the period leading up to the letter the Vatican seemed to be moving slowly towards acknowledging its own moral responsibility in the protection of clergy child abusers. In the meantime, the clergy sexual abuse scandal had moved to Germany and questions were being asked with regard to the extent of Pope Benedict's involvement in the case of a paedophile priest while Archbishop of Munich. In this climate the Vatican seemed to have switched to a more defensive position in coming to terms with its own moral responsibility. This consideration needs to be borne in mind in reading the pastoral letter.

The letter was issued on Saturday 20 March 2010 and was to

be read at all Masses the following Sunday. The strength of the letter is the pastoral stance adopted by the writer. At the outset, Pope Benedict explains his objective in writing the letter, as in order 'to express my closeness to you and to prepare a path of healing, renewal and reparation' (Par. 2). He addresses directly the victims of abuse and their families: 'You have suffered grievously and I am truly sorry. I know that nothing can undo the wrong you have endured. You have been betrayed and your dignity has been violated ... I openly express the shame and remorse that we all feel' (Par. 6).

The apology has historical significance. It is also probably one of the most direct and sincere papal apologies ever issued. As the head of the Catholic church, Pope Benedict goes on to reprimand his fellow bishops for their failures in leadership: 'It cannot be denied that you and your predecessors failed, at times grievously, to apply the long-established norms of canon law to the crime of child abuse. Serious mistakes have been made in responding to allegations' (Par 11). In hindsight I wonder will the Pope realise that his mistake was to stop there. His letter would have had much greater impact if he had gone on to acknowledge his own and his predecessor's failings in leadership in addressing this issue. The writers of a recent article in *Time* magazine entitled: 'Why Being Pope Means Never Having to Say You're Sorry,' pointed out the Pope in his letter was merely apologising for errors committed by the hierarchy of Ireland but not for anything he or the Vatican may have done (Jeff Israely & Howard Chua-Eoan, *Time* Magazine, 7/06/2010, 23). Professor Gerard Mannion, speaking at the *Broken Faith* conference at Milltown Institute in Dublin, aptly described this as the strategy of 'negative subsidiarity'. The focus is put on the local church and its failings in order to deflect attention from the failings of the central authority. Denis Bradley, who among his many roles is a management consultant, has noted that the tone of the letter was one of 'strategic distancing in times of difficulty' rather than an honest admission of culpability (2010, 4). The laity were not buying into this strategy as can be seen from an article in *The Irish Times* by Bishop Seamus Freedman reporting on written responses from over 3,000 Catholics to the bishops on the Pope's letter. They expressed disappointment 'that child sex abuse was not seen as a symptom of shortcomings in church structure and function' (*The Irish Times*, 28/12/2010).

The letter has also been criticised for seeking to blame 'outside' forces, for example secularism, for the clergy abuse scandal rather than acknowledging the role of 'inside' forces such as the culture of secrecy and protection that contributed to the cover-up. The nearest Pope Benedict gets to this is when he alludes to 'a tendency in society to favour the clergy and other authority figures'. (Par 4). The wording here is significant, he attributes the tendency to 'society' while we also know that this tendency resides in the clerical culture which seeks to protect the status of the priest. In fairness, the Irish bishops in their initial statement following the Murphy Report attempted to give some acknowledgment to the existence and impact of this culture.

Pope Benedict, by adopting a pastoral tone, attempted to draw close to his audience, but his failure to accept any personal responsibility only served to distance him from that same audience. This may account for the low level of satisfaction with the response of church leadership to the Murphy Report expressed in the Ipsos / MRBI Poll published in *The Irish Times* (11%) and in my own research reported in the Appendix. I find myself making a link between the initial responses to victims when they first came forward with allegations and the present response by the Vatican to reports detailing the cover-up that ensued. In both situations the response has been inadequate and has been marked by defensiveness on the part of church authorities.

There does seem to be a move away from the defensive stance of blaming the crisis on the media or on the presence of homosexuals in the priesthood, towards an acknowledgment of the internal and systemic factors that contributed to the crisis. However, this acknowledgment is often vague and nondescript. For example, Pope Benedict on a recent pilgrimage the Shrine of Our Lady of Fatima in Portugal made himself available to answer previously submitted questions from the press in his plane. Asked if the message of Our Lady of Fatima could be extended to covering the suffering of the church today, he answered: 'The suffering of the church also comes from within the church, because sin exists in the church ... The greatest persecution of the church doesn't come from enemies on the outside but is born in sin within the church' (*The Irish Times*, 12/05/2010). His reference to the persecution of the church coming from within seems a reversal of his *from without* articulated as late as 2002 when he was Prefect of the Congregation for the Doctrine of the Faith. On 30 November 2002, during a visit to the Catholic University of St Anthony in Murcia, Spain, in the course of a question and answer session he stated: 'I am personally convinced that the constant presence in the press of the sins of Catholic priests, especially in the Unitedf States, is a planned campaign.' Of even more significance is his acknowledgment that sin exists in the church. Does this imply that the church as an institution is sinful or is he inferring that it is merely individuals in the church who are sinful? This has major theological implications which I will take up again in chapter five.

A Glimpse at How the Irish Church Functions
The attempts made on the part of the bishops in the Irish church to respond to the crisis has given us a unique glimpse into how the church functions. The church is seen by the faithful and society at large as one coherent structure. Yet in the aftermath of the scandal it was seen to be disjointed and confused. Breda O'Brien, who writes from the stance of an informed and committed Catholic, observed how the crisis has revealed 'the dishevelled and incoherent nature of church structures'. She notes that the church in Ireland, consisting of dioceses and religious congregations, is made up of one hundred and eighty four parts and no one seems to be in overall charge (2010, 84). The governing structure is one where each bishop is autonomous in his diocese and directly accountable to the Pope. Religious orders and congregations require the permission of the local bishop to work in his diocese but are answerable to their own leadership for their internal affairs. The popular perception among the media and the people in the pews is that the conference of bishops possesses legislative power in its own region and should be able to initiate and coordinate a response to any given problem but this is not the case. Its legislative powers are limited by the prescriptions of Canon Law (Canon 455). The body representing Irish priests, the NCPI was disbanded a number of years ago. In the aftermath of the Murphy Report there was no representative

group to speak on their behalf. On 16 September 2010 over 300 priests turned up in Portlaoise for the inaugural meeting of the newly formed Association of Catholic Priests which aims to provide a voice for the clergy on issues that arise in the church and in society (*The Irish Times*, 17/ 09/ 2010).

Pope Benedict XVI and the Sexual Abuse Crisis
Pope Benedict's involvment in the clerical sexual abuse crisis can be seen as occuring in three phases: his role as Archbishop of Munich (1977-82), as Prefect of the Congregation for the Doctrine of the Faith (1982-2005) and as Pope (2005-present). (The noted Vatican commentator and *National Catholic Reporter* columnist John L. Allen Jr.*) The first period relates to his time as Arcbishop of Munich. During that period he had some involvement in the case of Fr Peter Hullermann. Archbishop Ratzinger had approved his transfer to Munich for therapy where it was known that he had sexually abused children in his previous diocese. Hullermann was later given a pastoral assignment in Munich where he went on to commit further acts of abuse for which he was convicted in 1986. The Vicar-General of the Archdiocese at the time has taken full responsibility for this decision. However, since Ratzinger was archbishop, he bore ultimate responsibility.

A more extensive series of questions relate to Cardinal Ratzinger's role as Prefect of the Congregation for the Doctrine of the Faith (CDF). In 2001 Pope Paul II issued a *motu proprio* entitled *Sacramentorum sanctitatis tutela* instructing all bishops to send cases of priests accused of child sexual abuse to the CDF thus transferring responsibility for the handling of such cases from the local church to the Vatican. Questions relating to this period concern the case of Fr Lawrence Murphy accused of molesting as many as 200 deaf children while working at a school from 1950 to 1974. Requests for the laicisation of Fr Murphy were sent from the United States Bishops to Cardinal Ratzinger but no action was taken at the time.

John L. Allen Jnr, who has made a study of Pope Benedict's

* http://ncronline.org/ news/accountability/credibility-gap-pope-needs -to-answer-questions

handling of the crisis, speaks of the then Cardinal Ratzinger undergoing 'something of a conversion experience' through 2003-2004. He claims that during this period the CDF became 'the beachhead for an aggressive response to the sexual abuse crisis'.*

Perhaps the best illustration of this change in Cardinal Ratzinger's stance involves the case of Mexican priest Marcial Maciel Degollado, the high profile founder of the Legionaries of Christ, against whom allegations of sexual abuse had been in the public forum for over a decade. In 1998 a group of former members of the Legionaries filed a canonical complaint with the CDF. It was not until 2001 that a formal investigation was launched. No action was taken against Maciel for the next four years. A year after his election as Pope, in May 2006, Pope Benedict took the step of barring Maciel from public ministry, instructing him to live a life of prayer and penance. Due to his advanced age no formal canonical trial was held. However, the Pope's decision sent a clear message. According to John L. Allen Jnr, his decision was 'widely taken as proof of a new dispensation in the Catholic church: If you're credibly accused of abuse, no power in heaven or earth will protect you from paying the price.' In the same year the Congregation for Bishops announced that a modified version of the 2002 American norms for sexual abuse, including the 'one-strike' policy, had been permanently approved. According to Allen this marks the transformation of Pope Benedict into a supporter of the 'zero tolerance' policy.

Many local bishops, who may have experienced difficulties in dealing with the Vatican on the clergy sexual abuse issue, are willing to give credit to Pope Benedict for breaking the wall of silence and demonstrating that there is no place in ministry for clergy convicted on the sexual abuse of children. However, many Catholics are left wondering why it took so long to face up to the issue. In assessing Pope Benedict's attempts to deal with the crisis, John L. Allen Jnr gives him credit for dealing with level one of the problem – subjecting abusers to the strictures of canon law, reaching out to victims and apologising for the suf-

---

* http:// ncronline.org /news / accountability / will-ratzingers-past-trump-benedicts-present. Accessed 5/07/2010

fering they have endured. However, the problem at level two still needs to be addressed. This will involve embarking on an indepth study of the causes of clergy sexual abuse and the failure of church leaders to adequately respond to complainants. There is also the issue of accountability. So far Pope Benedict has not adopted any new accountability mechanism for bishops. While offending priests have been taken out of ministry, few bishops have been asked to resign. In conclusion, I think the following assessment by John L. Allen Jnr is both fair and accurate: 'As long as the perception is that the Catholic Church has fixed the priests' problem but not its bishops' problem, many people will see that job as half done.'*

On his recent visit to Scotland and England, Pope Benedict addressed the issue of clerical sexual abuse on four occasions. On the papal flight to Edinburgh he answered pre-submitted questions from journalists. He acknowledged that 'even the authority of the church was not vigilant enough, nor sufficiently fast and decisive when it came to taking the necessary measures.' (*Irish Times*, 17/09/2010). This would seem to be an admission that failure by church authorities to respond promptly to the problem led to a continuation of the abuse and an escalation of the problem. In his reference to 'the authority of the church' can we surmise that he is referring to local bishops or to the Vatican – or to both? During Mass at Westminster Cathedral (18/09/2010), he apologised for 'the immense suffering caused by the abuse of children especially within the church and by her ministers'. He went on to describe these acts as 'unspeakable crimes' (*The Tablet*, 25/9/2010). The use of the word 'crimes' rather than 'sins', which was the term used in his pastoral letter to the Irish church, suggests an acknowledgment that these acts constitute a crime in civil society and need to be dealt with by the criminal justice system. In a column written in *The Guardian* following the Pope's visit, the playwright Bonnie Greet noted that 'giving justice to the victims of predator priests, and healing them, is the main job of his pontificate, whether he and his advisors accept this or not' (*Guardian*, 20/09/2010). I wonder whether, beginning his pontificate, Pope Benedict saw this as

* http:// ncronline.org /news / accountability / will-ratzingers-past-trump-benedicts-present. Accessed 5/07/2010

one of his top priorities. Whether he did or not, it is turning out to be the case.

Accountability and the Murphy Report

One of the first people to raise the issue of accountability following the publication of the Murphy Report was Archbishop Martin on a *Prime Time* programme on RTÉ. One may speculate as to why he chose to raise the issue in this forum. My guess is that he was concerned about credibility. The archbishop rightly perceived that if the church was to have a chance of regaining some of its credibility with its own membership and in the wider society, then the question of accountability needed to be faced. He also indicated that this was a personal issue for him as he would have difficulty sitting on committees with people mentioned in the Report who failed to publicly account for their stewardship. The archbishop's statement left the public waiting for individual bishops to address criticisms made in the Report. I don't intend to embark on a detailed analysis of their responses. Suffice it to say that they clearly struggled to address the question of accountability. Bishop Moriarty received widespread public support for the manner in which he explained his decision to resign, particularly for his readiness to accept shared responsibility. 'I accept that, from the time I became an auxiliary bishop, I should have challenged the prevailing culture.' (*The Irish Times*, 23/12/2009). In this short sentence he acknowledged: i) the existence of a culture of secrecy and protection and ii) that he had a responsibility to challenge it and so shares in a collective responsibility for harm that ensued. In reviewing how church leadership dealt with sexual abuse allegations, David Quinn concludes that bishops who had been appointed before the mid-1990s almost certainly were deficient in dealing with abuse allegations. Such bishops, if they fell below the standard set by the Murphy and Ferns reports should, in his view, resign. (2010, 336) He makes the point that if bishops were to voluntarily offer their resignation, without media pressure, this might be a powerful sign that lessons have been learned from the past. I think that the publication of the Framework Document in 1996 can serve as a cut-off point in coming to a judgement about bishops' moral responsibility. From that date there were clear guidelines for church leaders to follow. Those found to be in breach of those guidelines should consider their position. In a country where politicians and business leaders are notorious for their failure to accept any individual or collective responsibility, it would be refreshing to see church leaders with the moral courage and clarity to take such a step.

Bishop Moriarty's decision, and most particularly his line of reasoning, raises questions for leaders at all levels of church governance as to their level of responsibility for failures to respond adequately to clergy abuse allegations. Indeed, it raises questions for anyone working in an institution, whether school, bank or hospital. What responsibility does one bear for failing to challenge a culture that facilitates or tolerates wrongdoing? Enda McDonagh, writing in *The Furrow*, addressed the question of whether bishops found negligent in their dealing with sexual abuse allegations should resign. A bishop (*epi-scopi*) is an overseer, a supervisor. If their negligence in this role led to children being abused then they should resign (*The Furrow*, January 2010, 19). In this matter it needs to be acknowledged that bishops and auxiliary bishops bear different levels of responsibility.

Fr Patrick Hannon, professor emeritus of moral theology at Maynooth, deserves credit for addressing the complex question of collective responsibility (*The Furrow*, June 2010). Collective responsibility refers to a situation where wrong is done under the aegis of an institution. Blame is laid on those who share in the institution's governance. According to Fr Hannon, this applies especially in cases where 'the person enabled or facilitated the wrong, or could have prevented it.' (2010, 331). It may be that such a person has not done anything immoral or illegal yet their shared decision may have contributed to harm. It goes without saying that if one is to be held accountable then one must have had a say in the outcome (Hannon 2010, 335).

If one is to go by reports of inquiries into the HSE and other governmental bodies in Ireland, one would get the impression that once there is collective responsibility then no one is responsible. Patrick Hannon points out, 'systemic failure' must not distract from the fact that it was decisions of individuals that caused the wrongdoing (2010, 337). It is one thing to establish collective responsibility. It is another to conclude that the person bearing such responsibility should resign. In this situation one has to weigh up the 'sign value' of a resignation against the good an individual may be able to accomplish if he/she was to remain in their post (Hannon 2010, 337). This is very pertinent when one considers the calls on Cardinal Seán Brady to resign his post. In March 2010 Cardinal Brady acknowledged that in 1975 he was involved in a canonical investigation concerning sexual abuse allegations against Fr Brendan Smyth. This investigation involved interviewing two young people. In accordance with the requirements of a canonical inquiry, Fr Brady swore both complainants to secrecy. While it is acknowledged that Fr Brady performed the duties of his role and communicated the finding to his bishop, it is regrettable that this matter was not subsequently reported to the civil authorities in the light of the fact that Fr Smyth continue to abuse children for a further 18 years. An Ipsos/Mrbi Poll published in *The Irish Times* reported that 76% of people interviewed thought Cardinal Brady should resign, 15% thought he should not and 9% stated they didn't know (*Irish Times*, 14/06/2010). Applying the criteria identified by Patrick Hannon one could ask would the sign value of Cardinal Brady's resignation outweigh the value of the positive contribution he could make if he were to continue in his leadership role?

Whatever about resignations, there is no doubt that there is a need for repentance and reparation on the part of all those who had an overseeing role in the church while wrong was being done (Hannon 2010, 337). Holding leadership accountable is a key issue in resolving the clergy sexual abuse crisis. However, some commentators point to the fact that resignations of themselves do little to change the system. According to this view, priority should be given to changing the culture and the structure that contributed to the problem in the first place (Sean Ruth in Littleton & Maher 2010, 105).

In this chapter I have documented the development of the sexual abuse crisis following the publication of the Murphy Report. My attention has focused largely on the role of church leadership both in Ireland and in the Vatican. One gets the sense that, while progress has been made and the voice of victims is beginning to be heard, the problem so far has largely been responded to on one level only. The systemic issues that con-

tributed to the problem and the question of leadership accountability have yet to be adequately addressed. As I review events I
call to mind a statement made by the Australian Bishop
Geoffrey Robinson in 2007:

> I must confess my profound disappointment that no pope
> has so far said 'sorry' directly to all the victims and no pope
> has so far made a public promise urgently to study the caus-
> es of abuse and ruthlessly to change anything that might
> have contributed to abuse (2007, 221).

I hope Bishop Robinson is gratified to see the appearance of a
papal apology and to witness the Pope's willingness to meet
with victims of clergy abuse. However, he has yet to await the
emergence of a public promise to study the causes of abuse and
the systemic cover-up that followed. I wonder does the current
apostolic visitation of the Church in Ireland constitute such a
promise? What has become clear as I traced the developing nature
of this crisis is the emergence of a series of interrelated issues.
First, there was the question of the extent and nature of the
abuse and the inadequate nature of the response in the first instance at local or diocesan level and later at the level of the
Vatican. Next came the question of accountability and whether
those found to be remiss in their handling of allegations whould
resign. A related issue was the complex question of corporate or
shared responsibility: To what extent can individuals be held responsible for decisions made by a group comprised of an archbishop and his auxiliary bishops?

Questions for reflection and conversation:
Do you agree with the central criticism of the Murphy Report
that the priority of church authorities in the Archdiocese of
Dublin was the maintenance of secrecy, the avoidance of scan-
dal and the protection of the reputation of the church rather
than welfare of children and seeking justice for victims?
Do you think the Irish bishops accepted this central finding of
the Report?
What do you appreciate about Pope Benedict's Pastoral Letter?
What was missing from the letter?
Do you agree with the view that bishops and congregational
leaders criticised in the Murphy Report should resign?

Do you think that bishops and congregational leaders who failed to follow correct procedures in dealing with child sexual abuse allegations should voluntarily resign?

CHAPTER FOUR

Looking for an Explanation

The clergy sexual abuse scandal in the Dublin Archdiocese and in other parts of the world has given rise to strong feelings on the part of victims, their families, Catholic laity and others not affiliated with the Catholic church. It has also given rise to questions. The formulation of questions is the key to arriving at some understanding as to the causes of this crisis. This is a pre-requisite for any adequate response. What follows is a series of such questions that hopefully can lead to a deeper level of understanding. Most of them begin with short words like why and how? For example:

> How did a number of priests in the Dublin Archdiocese come to abuse a significant number of children?
>
> How could decent and intelligent human beings such as bishops fail to give priority to the protection of vulnerable children?
>
> Where was their moral sense of outrage as they listened to reports of abuse by their colleagues?
>
> How could they put institutional protection before the gospel demands of justice and compassion?
>
> Is there some institutional dysfunctionality at the heart of the church that might explain this scandal?
>
> To what extent have the systems, structures and culture of the clerical state contributed to the scandal?

At one time or another I expect the readers of this book have asked themselves one or other of these questions. The full range of questions is being asked now as the details of the clergy abuse scandal come to light. It is important that these questions be asked by those at different levels of leadership in the church, bishops, priests and laity. The text of a Pentecost Letter written in 2010 by an Australian Archbishop Mark Coleridge gives cause for hope and demonstrates a developing understanding of how the culture of the church facilitated abuse. In the letter he narrates the story of his growing awareness of the developing sexual abuse scandal. The first case he encountered was in the 1970s when he was a young priest in Melbourne. More cases came to light in the 1980s and 1990s, by which time he was serving as a spokesman for the church in Melbourne. He admits that at this stage he could not accept that this abuse was cultural – that it was more than merely personal, that it was the product of a 'system' (*Origins* 2010, 50). At the time he seems to have subscribed to what has become known as the 'bad apple' theory. This theory is based on the assumption that abuse comes entirely from outside the ecclesial system. The argument presumes that priests who abuse minors have infiltrated the priesthood and contaminated all the good apples in the barrel (Richard Sipe 2003, 256). Archbishop Coleridge goes on to describe how he came to work in the Vatican from 1997 to 2002, and it was only then that he began to seriously consider whether or not the abuse crisis was cultural in the church. He then started to ask the question: 'What was it that allowed this cancer to grow in the body of the Catholic church, not just here or there but more broadly?' (*Origins*, 2010, 52). He has now reached the stage where he is asking the systemic question.

The best service one can do for the church at this point in time is to insist on asking the systemic questions. It is only by doing so that we will be able to assist the church to come face to face with all the dimensions of the crisis and to embark on a realistic programme of renewal. Clergy sexual abuse occurs in a systemic or structured context and is not merely the result of a few bad apples in the barrel, however discomforting one may find that thought (Anton Shupe 2007, 6).

Various theories have been put forward to explain clergy sexual abuse. Fran Ferder and John Heagle made a list of them which I have amended.

Theories to Explain the Clergy Sexual Abuse Crisis:
- The Ancient History Theory
- The Rotten Fruit Theory

- The 'Gays Did It' Theory
- The Media Conspiracy Theory
- A problem confined to the 'English speaking world'
- The Lax Morals Theory
- The Celibacy Theory
- The Abuse of Power Theory
- Systemic Theory: Culture of Denial, Clericalism and Absence of Accountability

(Adapted from Fran Ferder & John Heagle. 'Clerical Sexual Abuse: Exploring Deeper Issues,' *National Catholic Reporter*, 10/05/2002, p 6-7)

You will notice that the first six theories on the list all attribute the blame to 'outside' influences. These are the ones favoured by those who resist acknowledging the systemic factors. There can be no adequate exploration of the crisis without adopting a systemic approach. I will now explore this as I treat of the systemic or cultural factors theory.

A Systemic Approach

In this approach, rather than isolating one factor in the crisis, a number of factors are considered simultaneously as they interact within a dynamic system. St Paul could be said to have taken a systemic approach in his description of the church as a body consisting of many parts. 'Just as each of our bodies has several parts and each part has a separate function, so all of us, in union with Christ, form one body, and as parts of it we belong to each other' (Rom 12:4). The church consists of many parts – a hierarchy with various sub-groups and the laity. While each part has a different function they are all interconnected. When one part misbehaves, the whole body suffers. Social scientists have taken a similar systemic approach to their study of families. Using the analogy of a family one could draw a comparison between sexual abuse in a family system and sexual abuse in a church family. In both situations similar dynamics are operative (Hidalgo 2007, 67). In sexually abusive families, also referred to as incestuous families, the system is characterised by an imbalance of power leading to control and domination. Both systems are characterised by a culture of denial and secrecy leading to rigid boundaries. People who grow up in abusive families learn that 'love is demonstrated by protecting family members from the wrath of outsiders' (Grant 1994, 183). A similar reluctance to engage with civil authorities was evident in the church. In abusive families the needs and expectations of a parent take precedence over those of a child (Grant 1994, 15). The same happened in the abusive church family. Both systems respond in a similar way to revelations of sexual abuse. Frantic attempts are made to protect the perpetrator and to try and maintain the *status quo*. In both systems revelations lead to loss of equilibrium and disturbance of the *status quo*.

Cultural/Systemic Factors

Culture is not an easy term to define. It has been pointed out that it is often those who are in a minority position in a particular culture, for example black people in a predominantly Western culture, who are the ones with a heightened awareness of the impact of culture on their lives. A definition by the American Jesuit George Wilson highlights the impact culture has on all our lives: 'A culture is a power-filled reality that conditions the ways people in a given social system will tend to think and behave' (Wilson 2008, 3). As we explore the abuse scandal we are interested in how the culture of the Catholic church shaped the behaviour of clergy abusers and church leaders in how they dealt with victims' complaints. I will be making frequent reference to a clerical culture which is the ecclesial world in which priests and bishops live. It has been described by Donald Cozzens, a priest/psychologist and seminary rector, as a world of 'preferment, exception and privilege.' (Cozzens, *The Tablet*, 5/12/2010, p 7). There is a growing consensus that this clerical culture has contributed in no small way to the toleration of sexual abuse and its subsequent cover-up (Sipe 2003, 260). This clerical culture breeds what has been called clericalism. It is 'grounded in the erroneous belief that clerics form a special elite and, because of their powers as sacramental ministers, they are superior to the laity' (Doyle 2007, 147).

One could describe a culture as the water we swim in. Often like the fish in the water, we swim around oblivious to its impact on us. Only when we see it described do we become conscious of its secret influence. Observers of Catholic culture warn us against viewing a clerical culture as being generated only by the clergy (Wilson 2008, 7). Church culture is the product of every-one affected by it. All Catholics have been affected by it to some degree and contribute to its maintenance. George Wilson points out that not every diocese is shaped by the clerical culture in the same way or to the same degree (2008, 69). I am sure that many Catholics from personal experience can attest to the truth of this statement. In chapter one, when discussing what it means to be Catholic, I talked about Catholicism as a form of individual and group identity. For the clergy, the clerical culture functions to shape an individual priest's sense of personal and group identity. This corporate identity gives to the individual an experience of inclusion within a group that has public standing in society (Wilson 2008, 15).

What about lay people and the clerical culture? Not every lay person is oppressed by the clerical culture in the same way. Those referred to as pre-Vatican II Catholics may be more shaped by it than post-Vatican II Catholics. My use of the word 'oppression' is intentional. Clericalism can function as a form of 'internalised oppression' for the laity, preventing them from finding their voice in the church and functioning as adults there (Sean Ruth 2006). It can be instructive to reflect on how the cleri-cal culture affects us. Chief among its many effects is that it tends to foster a stance of deference – deference on the part of laity to clergy, deference of priests to bishops and of religious to their superiors, and finally deference on the part of bishops and religious superiors to Vatican authorities.

Another avenue from which to explore the culture of clerical-ism is to try and spell out the assumptions underlying it. George Wilson has attempted to articulate these assumptions. They in-clude such beliefs as:

- Priests are all-holy; they are not subject to the spiritual and emotional infirmities that beset the rest of humanity
- Because they are ordained they are not accountable to society the way other citizens are
- Since they are the 'shepherds' of the faithful they are not re-quired to be accountable to them

- Canon law takes precedence over civil law
- The church and the ordained person should be protected from scandal

(George B. Wilson 2008, 31)

Cognitive psychologists such as Aron Beck have for the past thirty years been pointing out to us how cognitions (assumptions) influence behaviour. It doesn't take a genius to read through the assumptions outlined and realise the extent to which they gave rise to the behaviours criticised in the Murphy and other reports.

How is Church Culture Described in the Reports?
The culture of an organisation is reflected in its structures and procedures. The Murphy Report concludes that the 'structures and rules' of the Catholic church facilitated the cover-up in the Archdiocese of Dublin (Par. 1. 113). It is not surprising that reference to culture occurs with great frequency in a whole series of reports into clergy sexual abuse. The Ferns Report (2005) notes that 'a culture of secrecy and a fear of causing scandal informed at least some of the responses that have been identified by this inquiry' (2005, 256). The Murphy Report states that this 'culture of secrecy' was widespread. It operated not just in the Dublin Archdiocese but was also identified by the Attorney General for Massachusetts in the Archdiocese of Boston (Par. 1. 26). One readily makes the connection between the culture of secrecy and the abuse cover-up. We should also remember that it was this same culture which allowed the abuse to happen in the first place, where abusers used their position as clerics to give them access to children, and following the abuse demanded a promise of secrecy from their helpless victims.

In 2002 the American Bishops established a Review Board to look into the causes of the crisis. Between December 2002 and January 2004, the Board conducted 60 separate interviews with more than 85 individuals including cardinals, bishops, priests, theologians, victims, psychologists, lawyers and other knowledgeable people. On 27 February 2004 they published their findings under the title: *A Report on the Crisis in the Catholic Church in the United States* and referred to as the *National Review Board*

(NRB) Report. The Report has limitations largely related to its research methodology. For example, it did not take into account how the beliefs of Catholicism may have contributed to the problem (2004, 16). Nevertheless, its findings 'offer a comprehensive overview of existing opinion from within the Catholic culture of the factors that may be related to the sexual abuse crisis' (Hidalgo 2007, 57). The report identified a number of factors that contributed to the crisis. Two of these refer directly to the influence of a clerical culture: i) unwarranted presumptions in favour of accused priests, and ii) reliance on secrecy and undue emphasis on avoidance of scandal (American Review Report, *Origins*, Vol 33, No 39, 11/03/2004, p 256). I make reference to this report because, unlike the other reports referred to, it comes from a body set up by the American bishops and could thus be described as an 'internal' as opposed to an 'external' report. Sadly, their systemic analysis has not been reflected in the Vatican's response to the crisis.

A Church in Denial
From the reports I have quoted, two words stand out as they describe church culture: one is denial and the other is secrecy. Denial along with the culture of secrecy has contributed in no small way to the crisis. All of us engage in denial at some level or other on a daily basis. For example, we may have a chronic health condition such as blood pressure or diabetes and we minimise the seriousness of the conditon. Denial exists on a personal level and on an institutional or organisational level. When wrongdoing is going on in an organisation the people involved are often in denial as to what is going on. They will engage in a defence mechanism known as rationalisation.

The story of the clergy sexual abuse scandal is marked by denial on the part of all those involved – the denial by the perpetrator, the denial by his fellow clergy, the denial by superiors, the denial by the Christian community and institutional denial at the highest level. The fact that the Murphy Report caused such shock waves in the community is evidence of the pervasive presence of denial. In order to illustrate the extent of this denial I present a break down of the different levels at which it operates.

Levels of Denial:
- Denial of the damage done to victims
- Denial of criminal activity on the part of an ordained person
- Denial of legal responsibility to report the issue
- Denial of the systemic/cultural factors that contributed to the abuse and its cover-up
- Vatican denial

The failure to meet with victims is evidence of denial on the part of bishops who attempted to distance themselves from those harmed by the abuse. Victims were regarded with suspicion and as potential adversaries. This closed door approach to victims is admirably captured by Jimmy McCarthy in a song aptly titled: *The Christian Telephone:*

Tongues of fire
Hearts of stone
No reply on the Christian telephone.
(*Hey-Ho Believe* album 2010).

Incidentally, he wrote this song having watched the movie *Song for a Raggy Boy*. In a similar vein, the journalist Colum Kenny used the image of a stone to describe the 'cold and inert' quality of the church's response (Kenny 2010, 41). I have noticed since the publication of the Murphy Report an increased willingness on the part of church leaders including the pope to meet with victims and listen with compassion. This is evidence of the further breaking down of denial. Credit must be given to both partners in this conversation. I know from having listened to personal disclosures how challenging it has been for victims to makes themselves vulnerable all over again as they engage in conversations with church representatives connected to their abuse. By and large the experience proves to be a further step on their journey towards healing.

The survivors of clerical sexual abuse have had the major role to play in the breaking down of denial. However, it would be remiss of me not to mention the role of the media. The first programme to bring the scandal to public attention was the *Suffer Little Children* programme on UTV which exposed the Fr Brendan Smyth scandal. Then there was the Prime Time programme *Cardinal Secrets*, produced by Mary Raftery, investigating the response to clergy sexual abuse in the Archdiocese of Dublin and later, the BBC documentary *Suing the Pope* about the abuse of victims by Fr Sean Fortune in the diocese of Ferns.

I am aware that many Catholics have struggled to under-stand how educated and informed people like bishops and religious superiors could blind themselves to the fact that the sexual abuse of a minor is a criminal offence and as such should be reported to the civil authorities. A mind-set reflects a culture. Initially, clerical mind-set viewed sexual abuse as a moral wrong and a matter for repentance and the sacrament of reconciliation (Confession). Later, a more psychological-therapeutic approach was adopted. However, the failure to see it as a crime and a matter for reporting to the civil authorities is evidence of the desire to protect the priest from the strictures of the law and the church from the ensuing scandal. No doubt, on an intellectual level some bishops may have known that such wrongdoings should be reported. However, denial set in as they rationalised their obligation to do so. Again there is evidence that such denial has broken down. In Ireland the norms set out in *Our Children Our Church* (2005) reinforces the requirements laid out in *Children First* which places an obligation on all adults and organisations to report child abuse to the civil authorities (Par. 6.4). It is only in recent times that the Vatican has issued a clear statement on the obligation to report alleged offences to civil authorities. In a document entitled *Guide to Understanding Basic CDF Procedures Concerning Sexual Abuse Allegations*, bishops are instructed that where allegations of clerical child sexual abuse are involved 'the civil law concerning reporting of crimes to the appropriate authorities should always be followed.' (*The Irish Times*, 13/04/2010). While this statement is to be welcomed, it does not go as far as saying that allegations should be reported to civil authorities whether the law requires it or not, in other words mandatory reporting.

On 17 January 2011 the *Would You Believe* documentary *Unspeakable Crimes* was broadcast on RTÉ. It presented evidence of a 1997 letter coming from the Papal Nuncio in Ireland Archbishop Luciano Storero to the Irish Bishops' Conference. The letter spoke of reservations 'of a canonical and moral nature' on the part of the Congregation for the Clergy with regard to the recommendation contained in the *Framework Document* that priests who abused children should be reported to the civil authorities. The programme also reported that at a 1998 meeting with Cardinal Castillon Hoyos, prefect of the Congregation for Clergy, Archbishop of Dublin Desmond Connell thumped the table in frustration as the cardinal defended the Vatican policy of safeguarding the rights of the accused priest. Later in 2001 Cardinal Hoyos was to write a letter to a French bishop congratulating him for not reporting a priest's abuse to the police (*Irish Examiner*, 17/01/2011).

Vatican Denial

In documenting the clergy abuse crisis it seems that the Vatican is playing catch-up with local churches and national episcopal conferences. In the early stages of the crisis the Vatican was less than supportive of local churches in the stance they were taking. It was courageous of the American Review Board to publicly criticise the Vatican in this matter:

> The Vatican did not recognise the scope or gravity of the problem facing the church in the United States and it rebuffed earlier attempts to reform procedures for removing predator priests. (*Origins*, Vol 33, No 39. 11/03/2004, p 663)

Further evidence of Vatican denial emerged over the Easter period 2010 when two senior church figures commented publicly on the crisis. In an interview in the Vatican newspaper *L'Osservatore Romano*, Cardinal Sodano accused the media of trying to transform the individual guilt of priest abusers into a 'collective guilt' imposed on the church. He implied that responsibility and blame belonged to those clergy who abused, so the church as a community bore no collective guilt (*The Irish Times*, 8/04/2010). This is a repeat of the 'bad apple' theory I mentioned earlier. Following on his heels, Cardinal Bertone tried to blame the crisis on the presence of homosexuals in the priesthood. This thesis was proposed by Vatican officials in 2002 when the crisis was at its height in the United States. I must confess to being shocked to see a high ranking Vatican official claim that there is a link between homosexuality and paedophilia. There is no credible evidence to support such a theory. In the words of Professor Harry Kennedy of TCD there is 'no special link between homosexuality and paedophilia and that is the plain science of it.'

Archbishop Martin, in his address *On the Future of the Church in Ireland* to the Knights of Columbanus in Ireland, made reference to 'strong forces which would prefer that the truth did not emerge'. He went on to speak about 'signs of subconscious denial on the part of many about the extent of the abuse which occurred.' Many commentators speculated where these forces of denial resided. Did they reside in Ireland, in the Vatican or in both places? (Denis Bradley, 2010, 4). I admire Archbishop Martin for drawing attention to the continued presence of denial. However, he is probably also aware that it takes a long time for a culture of denial to vanish from an institution in which it has been endemic.

Factors Contributing to a Culture of Abuse

At the start of this chapter I outlined the journey travelled by Archbishop Mark Coleridge as he tried to come to terms with the cultural and systemic factors that led to the crisis of clergy sexual abuse. As he set about exploring those factors he realised that no one factor makes the abuse cultural but rather a complex set of factors. He outlined them as follows:

- A poor understanding and communication of the church's teaching on sexuality, shown particularly in a rigorist attitude to the body and sexuality
- Celibacy
- Seminary training leading to 'institutionalised immaturity'
- Clericalism: understood as a hierarchy of power rather than service
- Triumphalism in the image of the church
- Giving priority to discretion
- An underestimation of the power and subtlety of evil

(*Origins*, 2010, 49)

He mentions clericalism as just one of the factors, implying that the culture that contributed to the abuse is broader than clericalism. He puts at the top of his list a poor understanding of the church's teaching on sexuality and a rigorist attitude to the body. He expands on this with reference to the Irish church and its contribution to the Australian church. What he says is so relevant that I take the liberty of quoting him at some length.

> We owe the Irish an immense debt of gratitude for what they have given us, but for complex historical reasons the church in Ireland was prey to the rigorist influence that passed from the continent to Ireland – often under the name of Jansenism – and found fertile soil there. It then passed into the Irish diaspora, of which Australia was part.' (*Origins*, op. cit., 2010, p 52)

Writers who have tracked the sexual abuse crisis which originated in Canada, the United States, Australia and Ireland have commented that all of those locations were served by Irish missionaries. In three of them the Irish Christian Brothers played a prominent role. The Ryan Report has made reference to the harsh, puritanical regime they set up in their schools. Their training and formation, like that of many Irish clergy and religious, contained strong elements of Jansenism. This illustrates how a particular theology can contribute in no small way to the creation of a culture. If the theology is defective then the resulting culture is toxic and thereby fosters an environment conducive to all kinds of abuse.

Organisational Culture and Group Think

If one wants to get a sense of an organisation's culture one can do no better than to go and observe a board or committee meeting. There one can see where the power lives, who defers to whom and how decisions are arrived at. The clerical culture of a diocese can be observed at deanery meetings and other gatherings of clergy. Complaints by victims of child sexual abuse first made their way to a reporting adult, then to the diocesan director of child protection, then to the bishop or religious superior and finally to an advisory group. The point I wish to make is that all complaints end up with a group and each group has a culture. This culture and the dynamics of the group will determine how the complaint is dealt with.

Theologian Paul Lakeland, who writes extensively on topics such as the church and the laity, makes the point that while the bulk of responsibility for the sexual abuse scandal lies with bishops and the clerical culture, due acknowledgment must be given to the role of the laity in upholding such a culture. He insists that we are either active opponents of such a culture or we are enablers (Lakeland 2009, 99). Just as bishops have been enablers of abuse in their tolerance of 'extracurricular sexual activities' (Sipe 2003, 260) on the part of clergy, the laity by adopting a deferential·stance to clergy have allowed them to continue to abuse their power in the way they have. Therefore the call to change that culture on the part of laity is a call to abandon deference and assume an adult stance in their relationship with the clergy. It involves holding them to account. Likewise, for priests and bishops the challenge is to create more egalitarian relationships with one another and with the laity. Such relationships are shaped by the interaction of both partners and change in relationship requires the action of both (Wilson 2008, 103).

One of the most valuable books published on the abuse crisis is *The Dublin/Murphy Report: A Watershed for Irish Catholicism?* edited by John Littleton and Eamon Maher. One of the contributors to this volumn is Sean Ruth, who has written extensively on leadership in organisations. In his article he draws on the research done by organisational psychologists, like himself, especially Irving Janis. He describes how Janis was fascinated by the way in which groups comprised of 'otherwise intelligent, well-meaning individuals who could make decisions that turned out to be unintelligent, immoral and dangerous' (2010, 103). This was one of the questions I posed at the beginning of this chapter. It also preoccupied the Commission of Investigation in the Dublin Archdiocese. In an effort to come up with an answer, Janis coined the term 'groupthink'. He defined it as:

> The mode of thinking that persons engage in when concurrence-seeking becomes so dominant in a cohesive in-group that it tends to override realistic appraisal of alternative courses of action. (Irving Janis 1971, quoted in Myers, David G., 2010, 291)

One might wonder how groupthink might operate in a diocesan group discussing allegations of clergy sexual abuse. The answer is to be found in the dynamic processes that underlie the phenomenon of groupthink (Ruth 2010, 103). Such a group comes to believe in its own inherent morality; because they believe themselves to be ethical they presume the decisions they make are ethical. Since they have been shaped to varying degrees by the culture of clericalism, they will unconsciously be drawn into a collective rationalisation. Undoubtedly there could be the odd person in the group experiencing discomfort who questions the consensus, however such a person would likely resort to self-censorship and in the end go along with the majority opinion. Prior to the adoption of *The Framework Document* in 1996, the group engaging in such deliberations would have been comprised almost entirely of clerics which would further reinforce the dynamics of groupthink.

This chapter has been an effort to arrive at some understanding of why the abuse occurred. I have chosen to concentrate on the systemic and cultural factors that contributed to the problem because I believe they move us away from focusing on the perpetrator to situating the problem in the context of the organisation and its culture. This approach has been advocated by a number of researchers who have studied the crisis, among them Marie Keenan who says: 'Most promising to me seems to be a systemic perspective which seeks explanations for sexual abuse by Catholic clergy in the complex interaction of many variables including social environment, specific organisational conditions, individual cognition and, of course, choice' (2010, 13).

For Reflection and Conversation:
What is your understanding of clericalism in relation to both clergy and lay people?
How prevalent it is in the church today?
How do you feel about the prospects for cultural/systemic change in the church?
Where do you see obstacles to such change?
What has the church done to regain some credibility with people like me and with the wider public?

CHAPTER FIVE

Will the Patient Accept the Diagnosis?

When we feel unwell, we follow a procedure of first going to the GP, then being sent for a series of tests etc, and finally going back to the GP to receive a diagnosis. In the previous chapter I have been subjecting the institutional church to a series of tests in an attempt to diagnose the root cause of the clergy sexual abuse scandal. The process will continue in this chapter where I will attempt to apply some standard diagnostic criteria which I hope will lead to a more accurate diagnosis of the problems besetting the Catholic church.

Signs of Narcissism
I can clearly recall those days following the publication of the Murphy Report which made reference to a culture of denial, of secrecy and of entitlement as widespread in the Dublin Archdiocese and saying to myself: this organisation is narcissistic. From my work as a therapist I was familiar with the criteria listed in the American Psychiatric Association's Manual (DSM-IV) for the diagnosis of narcissistic personality disorder. I was aware that these criteria were designed to apply to individuals, but I was applying them to an organisation and they seemed to fit. I list them as follows so you can see for yourself:

- Has a grandiose sense of self importance
- Believes he or she is 'special' and unique
- Requires excessive admiration
- Has a sense of entitlement
- Is interpersonally exploitative
- Lacks empathy
- Shows arrogant, haughty behaviours or attitudes
(*DSM-IV* 1994, 282).

Not surprisingly, these symptoms not only fit the profile of many of the priest abusers described in the Murphy Report, they also describe the culture of the organisation they worked for. Take, for example, the culture of denial. The church as an institution would seem to share with narcissists a reluctance to take responsibility for failures. When something goes wrong the narcissist is never to blame. He/she will project the blame onto others. Some of the theories explored in the previous chapter can be seen as attempts to project the blame onto others, for example: 'The Media Conspiracy Theory'; 'The Gays Did It Theory'; and 'The Lax Morals Theory'. The narcissistic tendencies of the institution were also evident in the way victims and their families were treated when they first came forward with allegations. It can also be seen in the struggle the church seems to have in acknowledging institutional sinfulness with respect to past wrongdoing.

Narcissistic Reluctance
The Catholic Church's struggle to come to terms with past wrongdoings came to light in the Millennium Year when Pope John Paul II celebrated a solemn liturgy in St Peter's where the cardinals of the Roman Curia joined him in offering a 'universal prayer' which had the title: 'Confession of Sins and Asking for Forgiveness.' This prophetic gesture and others like it were later to pose a theological problem. Did it imply that the church as such shared the guilt of those sins and if so, how could this be reconciled with the church's holiness? (Francis A. Sullivan, 2000, 18). The question was duly referred to a body known as The International Theological Commission (ITC) which eventually published a report entitled: *Memory and Reconciliation: The Church and the Faults of the Past* (2000). The solution the Commission offered was to distinguish between Holy Mother Church and her sinful children. 'It is only the latter holiness that is mixed with imperfection and sin.' (quoted in Sullivan, op.cit., p 19). So, should the church acknowledge its own sinfulness? The readers of the Murphy Report would answer with a resounding 'yes'. However, the theologians of the ITC advise against this. According to them the church 'confesses herself a sinner, not as a subject who sins, but rather in assuming the

weight of her children's faults in maternal solidarity, so as to co-operate in overcoming them through penance and newness of life' (quoted in Sullivan, op.cit., p 19). The Commission, in attempting to ascribe sinfulness to 'her children' who did things 'in contradiction to the gospel', ignores the fact that many of these children were not acting in a private capacity. They were implementing policies and practices in the name of the church. As the respected theologian Francis A. Sullivan has observed: 'What is needed is the frank recognition that some official policies and practices of the church have been objectively in contradiction to the gospel and have caused harm to many people' (op. cit., 2000, 22). I have gone into some detail in explaining the theological reasons for the church's reluctance to acknowledge its sinfulness, because it is behind Pope Benedict's failure to come forward and issue a full papal apology.

Narcissism: The Shadow-Side of the Organisation
Different disciplines have their own terminology to describe deviant behaviour. Ethics and moral philosophy speak of wrongdoing. Theology might describe such behaviour as sinful, and psychology might use the term egotistic or narcissistic. In the previous chapter I described the clerical culture and how it contributed to child sexual abuse and its cover-up. This clerical culture supported narcissistic tendencies in abusing priests and contributed to a culture of narcissism in the church itself (Doyle 2007, 154). When one speaks about the culture of an organisation one is speaking about the soul of the organisation. To describe the clerical culture as narcissistic may come as a shock to many Catholics who have a deep love for their church. Understandably, they may resist or question the diagnosis. However the behaviours warrant the diagnosis and one needs an accurate diagnosis if one is to come up with an effective treatment plan. The symptoms of this narcissism in the institutional church consist of the following:

- A culture of clericalism
- A 'holiness' theology/ideology
- Denial and cover up of sexual abuse of minors by priests
- Reluctance to take responsibility for failures to adequately

protect children
- Absence of a pastoral care response to victims of abuse and their families
- Over-reliance on legal advice leading to a confrontational approach to victims

A psychological diagnosis, no matter how accurate, cannot adequately describe the totality of a person. Likewise, the diagnosis of the church as narcissistic does not do justice to the totality of the church. However, it does point to where treatment is urgently needed. The behaviours I have outlined could be described as 'the shadow side' of the organisation. I borrow the term from Gerard Egan who has written extensively on helping relationships and then turned his attention to organisational issues. He refers to the shadow-side of organisations which consists of a hidden series of beliefs, values and norms that drive organisational behaviour and which often contravene the public stance of the organisation (Gerard Egan 1994, 9). Narcissism could be described as the shadow-side of the church which contravenes the caring and self-sacrificing stance it claims to aspire to.

Recommended Treatment
Paradoxical as it may seem, the primary therapists to the church are the very victims and survivors of the abuse scandal. A more theological way of putting it would be to say that the church is being 'evangelised' by the abused. (McDonagh 2010, 115). In telling their story through the various channels open to them (reporting allegations, meeting with church leadership, testifying to commissions, media appearances) they have been confronting (placing before) the church and society at large with the story of child abuse. In seeking restorative justice from the offending parties and campaigning for reforms, they are challenging the church to take them seriously, to move towards victim empathy and take responsibility for wrongdoing. As it turns out, these are all standard steps in the treatment of narcissistic personality disorder.

On a spiritual level, the standard treatment consists in a good dose of humility. Bishop Malcolm McMahon of Nottingham prescribed this in a recent radio interview on the BBC: 'We have to be seen as servants of the people, much more humble, much more down to earth' (quoted in *The Tablet*, 24/04/2010, p 36). On a theological level, the church needs to engage in a process of critiquing its own theology (ideology) in an attempt to identify unhealthy teachings which may have contributed to the culture of narcissism. In this context, it is worth pointing out that in several places the Vatican II Documents speak about the church as holy but at the same time in need of purification. Little did the authors of these documents realise that it would take a major scandal to bring home to the church the full acknowledgment of this truth.

The Church Functioning Like an Addictive Organisation

Once a crisis develops in an organisation, this exposes the organisation to public scrutiny and hopefully challenges the organisation to look at itself. Sometimes outside bodies are brought in to assist the organisation in doing this. The setting up of the Commission of Inquiry into the Dublin Archdiocese is an example of this. Helpful as these external reports may be, ultimately it is up to the organisation itself to engage in its own self-critique. I am conscious of this as I set about applying the diagnosis of an addictive organisation to a diocese or congregation in the Catholic church. Before I do so, I need to make the following reservations. Just as there is no such thing as an addictive family there is no such thing as an addictive organisation. A more accurate way to put it, would be to say that the family or organisation functions as an addict or displays addictive behaviours. Secondly, after twenty years working as a therapist I have come to the realisation that one cannot simply tell someone he/she is addicted. Ultimately they have to make this diagnosis for themselves. I can describe how an addictive organisation functions; however, it is up to each diocese or congregation to come to that conclusion for themselves. This is a prerequisite for engagement in any meaningful change.

What is an Addictive Organisation?

In describing the term narcissism, I pointed out that it was first applied to individuals and by extension it came to be applied to families, groups and organisations (Pressman & Pressman

1994). The same happened for the term addiction. In the early days, the term was applied to individuals who abused substances such as drugs and alcohol. Later, it came to be applied to individuals engaging in activities such as shopping, sex and work. Later again it came to be applied to organisations. Before going on to look at addictive organisations, I think it would be helpful to furnish you with a definition of work addiction. Bryan Robinson, in a book aptly titled *Chained to the Desk*, defines work addiction as:

> An obsessive-compulsive disorder that manifests itself through self-imposed demands, an inability to regulate work habits, and an overindulgence in work to the exclusion of most other life activities. (1998, 7).

Work addiction is perhaps the most socially acceptable of all addictions. For the work addict, existence can be said to be centred around work: 'I work therefore I am.' One should not be surprised to find religious professionals such as priests, who profess to live and work from a spiritual centre, to be vulnerable to work addiction. In fact, they may be more vulnerable than most since they don't have a marriage commitment and their vocation demands high levels of dedication and sacrifice. Work addiction may be an occupational hazard for that reason.

Ann Wilson Schaef and Diane Fassel, having worked for many years with individuals in addiction, began to apply the term to organisations. Having studied the addiction process as it applies to individuals, they applied the insights gained to explore how organisations become addictive. I am especially interested in their work because since the 1990s I have seen the patterns they outlined repeated in the Irish Catholic church at diocesan and congregational level. During those years as the crisis unfolded, anxiety levels seemed to rise; dioceses and congregations began to function in an increasingly addictive fashion.

The symptoms of an addictive organisation can be said to have become evident in the way dioceses and religious congregations functioned:

- The mission of the organisation gets denied, ignored or forgotten

- Corporate survival reigns supreme
- The workaholic environment becomes self-centred and has no boundaries
- Crisis management becomes the norm

(Bryan S. Robinson 1998, 199)

Many of the deficiencies on a leadership and management level referred to in the Murphy Report are described by Anne Wilson Schaef and Diane Fassel in their portrayal of how an addictive organisation functions:

- Engages in denial – a closed system, no one knows what is going on
- Practises cover-up in order to present a good image
- Operates from a 'scarcity model' – scarcity of resources is used as a rationalisation for not adhering to best practice guidelines
- Ethical deterioration where morality is compromised
- The organisation is preoccupied with control

(Anne Wilson Schaef & Diane Fassel 1990, 62-68)

It will not come as news to many readers that addictive organisations tend to be preoccupied with control. In the context of the sexual abuse crisis, initial strategies adopted by leadership were largely aimed at control. Decision making groups dealing with allegations were mostly made up of clergy; canonical investigations swore complainants to secrecy, ostensibly to protect the good name of the accused. There was no reporting of allegations to civil authorities. These are all behaviours of an organisation preoccupied with control.

Readers familiar with the literature on addiction will have come across the term co-dependency. It refers to behaviours of those close to an addict which serve to facilitate his/her addiction. They are, so to speak, pulled into a co-dependent relationship with the addict. A similar process happens in organisations whereby employees are pulled into a co-dependent relationship with the organisation who employs them and end up supporting its addictive behaviours (Michael Carroll 2004, 101). Church personnel who had to deal with sexual abuse allegations found that their integrity was often compromised as they went along with the cover-up strategies of the addictive organisation. I addressed this in the previous chapter when I described how the dynamic of groupthink operates in organisations.

Leadership in an Anxious System
The management of the clergy abuse crisis on a diocesan and congregational level bore many of the characteristics of crisis management. In fact, crisis management became the norm. Anxiety levels in leadership and in the system remained at constantly high levels.

There are understandable reasons as to why this was the case. After all, the system was closed and rigid and preoccupied with control. Revelations of clergy sexual abuse posed a threat to the system, hence the anxious response. When someone is anxious they lose the ability to think straight and their response becomes very reactive. In many dioceses and religious congregations, anxiety and reactivity became the order of the day. A congregational superior once disclosed to me that his most stressful time of the day was opening the post in the morning as he feared it would contain a fresh allegation against one of his confrères. Information around allegations was kept secret, ostensibly to protect the good name of the accused, but the underlying dynamic was to contain the anxiety that had entered the system. Eventually when these allegations became public, whatever calmness was there quickly left the system and it became highly anxious once again.

I find the family systems approach to leadership indispensable for understanding how church leaders functioned during the clergy sexual abuse crisis. Edwin Friedman, a Jewish Rabbi and a disciple of family systems theorist Murray Bowen, defined leadership as: 'the ability to stay relatively calm in the midst of an anxious system' (Friedman 1985, 27). The operative word in this definition is relatively. One can't help being anxious in the midst of an anxious system. However, if one is to give leadership, one needs to be able to think clearly and bring a calming presence to others. In order to do this, one needs to contain one's own anxiety and remain relatively calm. According to Friedman and Murray Bowen the ability to do this goes back to childhood and early family of origin experiences. They describe leaders who can do this as self-differentiated. The term is difficult to define but essentially it means the ability to be true to oneself while still maintaining emotional connection with others. I wish to put forward the thesis that church leaders who handled the sexual abuse crisis well were those who had a good level of self-differentiation. Those with low levels of self-differentiation allowed their anxiety levels to go out of control and became defensive, protective and reactive. Following the publication of the Murphy Report, a discussion has taken place around the qualities required of a bishop. We all have our own list. As my contribution to the debate, let me include the qualities of a self-differentiated bishop:

- Can manage tension between being true to themselves and furthering the mission of the church
- Can balance the need to care for self and to care for others
- Does not over-identify with his role
- Can live in an anxiety-generating environment and yet remain relatively calm

If one reads between the lines in the Murphy Report one can see how it comes to the conclusion that the leadership in the Dublin Archdiocese was not able to balance their obligation to protect vulnerable children with their obligation to further the mission of the church. They seem to have over identified with their role and failed to be guided by their sense of human compassion and justice. In their meetings they were subject to the dynamics of groupthink and failed to challenge the prevailing culture. Several bishops have made the excuse that they were on a 'learning curve' with regard to the issue of paedophilia and how to deal with it. I want to suggest that the problem goes much deeper than simply acquiring up-to-date information.

I began this chapter posing the question: will the patient accept the diagnosis? I have been on the receiving end of medical diagnosis and I know the spirit in which it is given is just as important as the information conveyed. To give a diagnosis one has to adopt an objective stance. This is not an easy matter when one is describing a member of one's family or for that matter one's faith community. I have set out to do so as a member of the community under scrutiny who respects those who have taken on leadership responsibility in the community and believes that the community and society is best served when the leadership of the community is held accountable for its stewardship. My chief preoccupation as I wrote this diagnosis was to be balanced and fair in what I attempted to say. I adopted a largely systemic approach to the crisis. This led me to focus on the culture of the organisation which I described as characterised by different levels of denial and a tendency to protect and privilege a sub-group in the system, namely, the clergy.

I went on to highlight narcissistic and addictive traits present in the organisation. I looked at the profile of those with leadership responsibility. Those who functioned well seemed to be those with good levels of self-differentiation who did not over identify with their role. This gave them a greater freedom to act out of their own humanity and core values and resist the pressures of conforming to the demands of a clerical system. Others with lower levels of differentiation over-identified with their role, lost touch with their own humanity and were guided in their responses by the need to protect the institution at all costs.

For Reflection and Conversation:
To what extent has the clerical culture supported narcissistic tendencies in the clergy?
To what extent does the church's response to the victims of sexual abuse by clergy reflect narcissistic tendencies in the institution?
Vatican II speaks of the church as holy and at the same time in need of purification. What aspects of church culture would you see as needing purification?
Do you agree that the church functions like an addictive organisation? How do you see the church functioning as an addictive organisation?
To what extent has anxiety and reactivity marked the church's response to allegations of child sexual abuse by clergy? What are the signs of this?

Questions for mid-point reflection:
As I come to the end of this chapter and at this mid-point in the book, I am conscious that I need to provide the reader with some space to simply pause and reflect on the material presented. The following questions are presented with this purpose in mind:
How has your understanding and opinions of the clerical sexual abuse scandal changed?
What difference does it make to your understanding of the church you belong to?
How does it change your understanding of your role in the church?
What do you consider to be the real issues that now need to be addressed in the church?

CHAPTER SIX

A Profile of Priest Perpetrators

I include this chapter because I imagine that some of the readers of this book may be wondering about the inner world of a priest who betrays a sacred trust and sexually abuses children. Are these men similar to other sexual offenders? Is there something in their history that predisposed them to offend in this way? Is paedophilia more prevalent in the priesthood than in other professions? Why did so many priests abuse minors? Was it due to environmental factors? Were there any systemic factors in the priesthood, e.g. lifestyle, clerical culture or celibacy that contributed to priests acting out sexually? In order to find answers to these questions I intend to consult a number of sources. These include: research studies into this population, studies by clinicians who have worked with this group and biographical writings by clergy sex abuse victims describing their experience.

In writing about priest perpetrators I am conscious that I am describing a group of men who, like myself, were raised as Catholics and who still belong to the Catholic family. In other words, I am talking about family members. I referred in chapter two to the tendency to distance. If there is one group inside the Catholic Church at this time that the Vatican, bishops, religious superiors, brother priests, religious and laity are attempting to distance themselves from it is the priest perpetrator group. Laicisation, like divorce, is an extreme form of distancing. Justified anger felt by fellow priests and religious is leading them to distance from the offending party and in many cases to sever all connection. In fairness, I should point out that priests themselves, once an offence has become public, tend to isolate themselves from former classmates and friends. They feel they have let these people down and are reluctant to make contact with them. Bishops and fellow clergy are a long way from forgiving the priest perpetrator. Understandably they have to work through a lot of anger and resentment. This is frequently compounded by the revelation of new allegations. In the absence of some degree of forgiveness the relationship is bound to remain distant and conflictual. Dioceses and religious congregations have spent vast sums of money on legal fees and in the treatment of priest perpetrators. They expend extensive hours in managing each case and yet the one issue that fails to get addressed is mutual forgiveness.

Before describing this group of men, I need to acknowledge that they are not easy to understand. There is a natural tendency to distance oneself from them. One sees this distancing in the tabloid headings referring to them as monsters, perverts and scum. Their crimes are so horrific and repulsive that one wants to keep one's distance from them. Secondly, understanding their sexual attraction to children and young adults is difficult to comprehend. They are a very difficult population to work with clinically. They engage in huge denial and rationalisation. This makes trust very difficult. I heard of a treatment centre where offenders, when they presented on their first day of treatment, were told: 'We don't trust you, but we do care.' It is not easy to care for someone you don't trust. It is not easy to stay in relationship with someone when you never know if they are telling you the truth. Trust is normally the basis of relationship and with this group it rests on a fragile foundation. I have great admiration for clinicians, lawyers, social workers and therapists who serve this population. They do so because they are committed to making the world a safer place for children. I hope that they also do so out of our common humanity. Every offender is our brother or sister and ultimately in need of our support.

Research Data on Abusive Priests

The most recent data on abusing priests comes from the John Jay College of Criminal Justice 2004. This study was commissioned by the United States Conference of Catholic Bishops to gather data on the sexual abuse of children by Catholic priests in the United States between 1950 and 2002. I will summarise the findings of the report under a number of headings. In doing so, I am drawing from an article, *Abusive Priests: Who They Were and Were Not* by Mary Gail Frawley-O'Dea and Virginia Goldner, published in a book edited by the same authors entitled: *Predatory Priests, Silenced Victims: The Sexual Abuse Crisis and the Catholic Church* (2007).

Number of Abusing Priests:
The John Jay research concluded that 5,214 priests were credibly accused of sexual abuse of minors between 1950 and 2000. This accounts for 4.75% of the priesthood. These numbers are probably low since 7% of dioceses and 29% of religious communities failed to provide data (2007, 26). Corresponding figures for Ireland are not available. The HSE set about conducting an audit but were informed in 2008 by the Irish bishops that they could not co-operate due to legal reasons relating to data protection. In 2009 the bishops requested the National Board for Safeguarding Children to conduct an audit. By 2011 the National Board had only completed a review of practices in three dioceses. The Board's chief executive Ian Elliott said he was informed by the bishops (their sponsoring body) in September 2010 that they had received legal advice not to co-operate with the review due to possible preaches of data protection legislation. Ian Elliott announced at the AGM of the National Board that these difficulties have now been addressed. The review would proceed but findings on child protection practices in dioceses and congregations may not be published without permission of a relevant bishop or religious superior (*The Irish Times* 12/05/2011). Without a proper audit is impossible to assess the extent of child sexual abuse by clergy and the compliance with child protection policies. It is instructive to compare the lack of progress in this matter in Ireland with the United States where the bishops made a commitment to an annual audit in 2002 and it was up and running by 2004. Data collected by the journalist David Quinn estimated that 4% of all priests in Ireland have been accused of abusing minors over a period of fifty years (David Quinn, *Irish Independent*, 28/10/2005).

Geographical Distribution of Abusers:
The figures given above are from a nationwide survey, so naturally the number will vary from diocese to diocese. In the United States, for example, the figure for the Archdiocese of Boston (10%) is about twice the national average.

In Ireland the Archdiocese of Dublin (67) and the diocese of Ferns (21) had the highest number of reported credible allegations (David Quinn, *Irish Independent*, 28/10/2005). According to Archbishop Martin, during the period 1940-2010 allegations or suspicions of sexual abuse were made against 90 priests of the Archdiocese and against 60 religious priests who held diocesan appointments (4/4/2011, Marquette Conference Address).

Perpetrators by Year of Ordination:
In the US from 1963 through 1980 the percentage of abusing priests per ordination class rarely fell below 6.0% and in some years (1973) rose to 9.0%. There is a notable decline in the figures for ordination years after 1984 but this could be due to the fact that it takes a considerable length of time for victims to come forward (2007, 29).

Dates of Birth:
In the John Jay study almost two-thirds of abusive priests were born before 1940 and almost 90% before 1950. Many of these priests would have entered minor seminaries at 14 or 15 years of age. (2007, 29).

Age of Priest at First Incident of Offence:
The average age of a priest at his first reported incident of sexual abuse was 39. This suggests that priests may have first begun to abuse about ten years after ordination. (2007, 30). This data has some significance since it disputes the myth that these men entered the priesthood in order to have access to minors. If this were true they would have set about their abuse soon after ordination. The research literature suggests that it's unlikely these men would have chosen the priesthood in order to have access to children (Keenan 2009, 204).

History of Personal Victimisation:
Only 6.8% of priests in the John Jay Study reported histories of childhood abuse. According to Frawley O'Dea and Goldner this figure may be understated (2007, 30). The figure stands in stark contrast to clinical evidence which estimates the number of priest abusers with childhood histories of sexual abuse to be as high as 50% (Grant 1994, Rossetti 1997, Sipe 1995) I will take up this question again when I report on clinical data.

Number of Victims Per Priest:
According to the John Jay Study 55.7% of credibly accused priests had only one victim; 26.9% had two or three; 13.9% had four to nine; and 3.5% had ten or more. These figures relate to the number of victims who came forward to accuse priests. They don't refer to the actual number of victims the accused priest abused. These figures are hard to come by, as offenders are notorious for under disclosure of victims.

Age of Victims:
The majority of victims were abused between the ages of 10 and 14. While girls were abused most frequently at ages 11 to 14 there is evidence over the decades of a shift towards male victims reporting abuse for the first time between 15 to 17 years of age (2007, 31). This data has important clinical significance which I will take up later.

Gender of Abuse Victims:
Of those abused 81% were male and 19% were female. Male victims tended to be older than females. In Ireland the SAVI Study found that clergy were more likely to have abused boys (5.8 percent of cases involved abuse of boys by clergy compared to 1.4% of reports involving abuse of girls by clergy) (Goode *et al* 2003, 25).

Abusive Acts:
Most abusing priests committed acts more serious than just touching under a victim's clothes (about 9%). About one third sexually penetrated their victims or engaged them in oral sex. Over half of those abused claimed to have been abused a number of times, while 29% claim to have been abused only once. (2007, 33). Another fact to emerge from the study was that in 21.6% of the cases the abuser priest was found to be using alcohol and/or drugs. This means that in a great majority of cases the abusing priest was clean and sober. This contradicts the defence put forward by abusers that alcohol or drugs were to blame.

Reporting to Civil Authorities:
Only 14% of the priests denounced to their bishops were re-

ported to the police. Of those reported, half were charged and most who were charged were convicted (John Jay College of Criminal Justice 2004).

Usually it is the case that we experience shock and revulsion as we listen to stories of abuse, but we can equally experience shock as we listen to the statistics. My motive in presenting the facts is not to shock but to dispel misconceptions surrounding clergy abusers. The data suggests that the extent of sexual abuse of minors by Catholic clergy is no greater than in the general population (Keenan 2009, 198). However, their victims tend to be older and to include a greater proportion of males. It goes without saying that the extent of child sexual abuse by Catholic clergy should ideally be less than in the general population. They aspire to high moral ideals, receive extensive education and training and take a vow of celibacy.

Clinical Data on Abusive Priests

When one compares priest and nonpriest sex offenders to the non offending population, on the surface they look the same. Furthermore, there is no single clinical profile that covers those who go on to abuse children. Likewise there is no clinical profile that covers abusing priests. When one reads the clinical data relating to abusive priests the most striking fact to emerge is that they are not all the same. They range from serious predators with hundreds of victims to wounded individuals with few victims who acted out under stress and abused. Each individual priest perpetrator can be placed somewhere on that continuum. In this context it is worth quoting the criticism of Marie Keenan with regard to the media presentation of clerical men who have abused children. They have been presented as 'a homogenised group, whose offending histories are the same, and all of whom represent continuous danger to children in every situation' (Keenan 2009, 194).

The typical adult sex offender is male, between the ages of eighteen and thirty-five, heterosexual, married and has a history of some form of physical or sexual abuse in childhood. He has poor impulse control and often has a history of antisocial behaviour (Hildalgo 2007, 39). Unlike typical sex offenders, most offending priests are older when they commit their first alleged offence. In the John Jay College Study we saw that the average age of a priest at the first reported incident of sexual abuse was 39 years. Furthermore, unlike typical sex offenders, priests generally display less anti-social behaviour and higher standards of social competence and self-control (Hildago 2007, 39). The findings of the John Jay Study and other research reveal a pattern where priests are more likely to offend against older children, have fewer victims, target male victims, and display greater sexual conflictedness than other child molesters (Hildago 2007, 39).

Clinical psychology has learned not to treat paedophiles as a homogeneous group and so it has arrived at certain clinical distinctions which serve as a guide in formulating treatment plans, establishing prognosis and making risk assessments. One of the most helpful clinical distinctions is that between paedophilia and ephebophilia. The distinction is based on the age of the abused child, 13 and below being the arbitrary cut-off for a paedophile diagnosis and 14 through to 17 for ephebophilia. Based on this distinction, we can conclude that not all abusive priests are paedophiles. In fact, a sizable proportion of them are ephebophile abusers (Kochansky & Cohen 2007, 36). The reason for saying this is that their victims are of a post-pubescent age. They are erotically drawn to adolescents as opposed to children. The media commonly refers to all priest sex abusers as paedophiles whereas their psychological dynamics and sexual preferences seem to be those of ephebophiles (Kochansky & Cohen 2007, 38). This distinction has important clinical implications as the treatment prognosis for the latter is much more positive. It is important to point out that not all child sexual abusers are either paedophiles or ephebophiles. There are some who don't meet the clinical criteria for such a diagnosis. About half of child molesters exclusively target children of a specific age group, while others are more flexible regarding the age of their victims (Hildago 2007, 39). According to Myra Hildago, the majority of priest child sex abusers would seem to have more in common with fathers who sexually abuse their own children or step-children than with other types of child molesters. Compared to other sex offenders, incestuous fathers are generally older, have fewer victims and demonstrate less antisocial behaviour and are more likely to have problems with sexual dysfunction, poor social skills and isolation (Hildago 2007, 40). On the other hand, what distinguishes priests from incestuous fathers is that they are not married and are more likely to abuse male victims.

Developmental History of Sexual Abusers
The developmental history of all sexual abusers shows evidence of arrested psychosexual development. A good number of paedophiles are found to be fixated at a certain stage of their psychosexual developmental. These tend to be exclusively attracted to children and when offending have a greater number of victims. The treatment prognosis for this group is not as positive as for regressed paedophiles who are sexually attracted to adults and to children, but when under periods of stress tend to regress to an earlier stage of development. Fixated paedophiles are often 'developmentally immature, passive, heterosexually inhibited, and deficient in sexual knowledge and social skills' (Kochansky & Cohen 2007, 40). In contrast the ephebophile's interest in older children usually reflects a higher level of social and psychosexual development (Kochansky & Cohen 2007, 40).

In reading details of abusing priest's offending history you will often find reference to the fact that they tend to get on well with children and could engage with them readily, displaying an interest in their hobbies and pursuits. One of the reasons for this is that they are often psychologically at a similar developmental stage and this gives them a facility in grooming their potential victims. To the outsider nothing may seem amiss except that on closer examination they may seem to invest more time in fostering friendships with young adolescent males than with their peers.

A History of Childhood Sexual Abuse
Looking again at the psychosexual development history of abusing priests there is evidence that many of these priests have themselves been subjected to premature sexual interactions with an adult as minors. This would have contributed to their arrested development and to a host of other psychological traits including repetitive compulsive sexual behaviours (Kochansky & Cohen 2007, 43). Depending on authors consulted, the estim-

ates vary between 30% and 80% (Keenan 2009, 205). I first came across a reference to this when I was reading a book by clinical psychologist Richard Grant entitled, *Healing the Soul of the Church: Ministers Facing Their Own Childhood Abuse and Trauma*, (1994). Based on his own clinical practice and discussions with colleagues, he suggested that up to 25% of men and women in clerical and religious life in the United States and Canada were the victims of childhood or adolescent sexual abuse (1994, 179). In the closed seminary environment this was never disclosed and remained an unhealed wound, an untreated trauma. This would have impacted on their psychosexual development. Depending on the extent of the abuse this could have resulted in fixated or regressed development. Later, as ordained priests or professed religious, a certain proportion of this group (approx. 50%) would have acted out by entering into inappropriate relationships and sexually abusing children and adolescents. In Grant's view 'the majority of untreated victims of childhood sexual abuse continue to either victimise or be victimised throughout their adult lives' (1994, 180). I must confess that I was somewhat shocked at the suggestion that 25% of seminarians had experienced sexual abuse. When one takes into account the level of childhood sexual abuse in Ireland, this figure may not be far off the mark. For example, the *Sexual Abuse and Violence in Ireland Study* (SAVI 2002), reported that 20% of women and 16% of men experienced sexual abuse involving physical contact in childhood while a further 10% of women and 7% of men experienced non-contact sexual abuse as children (Goode *et al* 2003, 23). If this is the rate of sexual abuse in the general population, why shouldn't it be somewhat similar for those who had entered seminaries? Unfortunately, we don't have any data as to the number of convicted priest abusers in Ireland who have been subject to sexual abuse in childhood. The data from the John Jay Study in the United States put the figure at 6.8%. As the estimate for males suffering sexual abuse in childhood is higher for Ireland than the United States, I would expect the figure to be higher for Irish priest abusers.

What conclusions can be drawn from the clinical data presented? First, the high figure for child sexual abuse in Ireland among males and females is indicative that child sexual abuse is located 'within the general adult population and not with a few individuals who are identified as monsters' (Marie Keenan 2009, 184). Secondly, any attempt to link paedophilia with clerical celibacy does not stand up. It wasn't celibacy that led ordained priests to be attracted to children. Rather it was their arrested psychosexual development. The disorder was there before they made any celibate commitment. Celibacy may have been an attractive option for such candidates as it provided them with a ready made solution to their conflicted sexual tendencies. I imagine it must be pretty disturbing for a young man to discover that he has a sexual preference for young male children and to assume that he wouldn't be accepted if people knew about his inclinations in this matter. Institutions like religious communities and the priesthood would have an instant appeal, promising a place of belonging and social esteem. 'Celibacy is so attractive to paedophiles because they want to leave their conflict-laden sexuality behind them and liberate themselves from their sexual impulses' (Klaus M. Beier, *The Tablet,* 13/03/2010, 9). A third conclusion is that priority should be given to providing a safe environment in seminaries and houses of formation where candidates are encouraged to seek healing and professional help for whatever wounds they carry. I have a concern that the present climate of zero tolerance and weeding out the sexually wounded, will make it difficult for seminarians in formation who might need professional help, to to come forward and request it.

Narcissism Among Priest Abusers
Besides arrested psychosexual development another personality feature common to abusing priests is the presence of traits consistent with narcissistic or dependent personality disorder (Kochansky & Cohen 2007, 42). I have already referred to narcissism in the previous chapter when I described the clerical culture as narcissistic. Here I want to make the point that candidates with narcissistic personality traits have been and will be drawn to the priesthood and to the clerical culture surrounding it. In today's climate it may not afford them the special status that it did in the past but it does afford them entrance into the clerical culture. We do best to consider narcissism as existing along a continuum, with each of us somewhere along that continuum.

Those with narcissistic personality disorder are to be found at the high end of the continuum. It is estimated that the disorder is to be found in about one percent of the population, more in men than in women (Duckro & Falkenhain 2000, 25). Certain dimensions of narcissism have been found among priest sexual abusers, notably the exploitative and entitlement dimension (Doyle 2007, 154). Victims of clergy sexual abuse attest to the manner in which they were discarded by their priest abuser after he had done with them and the complete disregard of their feelings and vulnerability. Narcissists can be not just manipulative but intimidating. Again when one reads the accounts of victims, one finds indicators of how the abusing priest intimidated not just the victims but the adults in the victim's family.

As one learns about the psychosexual and personality factors present in the make-up of priest child sexual abusers, it would be natural to think that the abuse is the result of a deficit in psychosexual development or an individual pathology present in the abuser (the bad apple theory) but it is much more complex than that. We need to remember that abuse, when it occurs, takes place within a social context. For example, it occurs within a family or within an institution (Marie Keenan 2002, 598). The abusing priest brings with him a certain vulnerability which interacts with environmental factors to bring about the abuse. This is where the culture of narcissism comes into play fostering 'self-serving attitudes and narcissistic personality traits in sexually immature clerics who then act with a sense of entitlement in exploiting their positions of trust with the laity' (Hidalgo 2007, 52). Len Sperry, who has studied the phenomenon of clergy misconduct, is of the opinion that it is the result of four intersecting factors: the person of the minister, institution or organisation dynamics, ministry assignment and relationships (Sperry 2003, 65). To blame the phenomenon of clergy misconduct on one of these factors, for example, the person of the minister, is unwarranted. All four have a bearing in every case of clergy misconduct. One feature to be borne in mind is that the presence of high levels of stress resulting from organisational dynamics has been found to have a bearing on ministers crossing sexual boundaries.

Victims Stories: A Profile of Priest Abusers
Victim's stories generally have two main characters, the abuse survivor and their abuser. The chief character tends to be the abuse survivor since he/she is the narrator of the story. It is this person that one comes to know through the reading of the story. The stories also contain valuable profiles of the priest abuser. I will present two stories here because I think they provide a graphic illustration of much of the clinical data described above. In the course of my professional life, I have read extensively on the subject of priest sexual abusers. The book that made the greatest impact was *Father and Me: A story of sexual abuse at the hands of a priest* (1995). It was the account of a young man's abuse by an Irish Catholic priest ministering in the diocese of Birmingham. The young man's name was Eamonn Flanagan and the priest who abused him over a twelve year period was Fr Samuel Penny. Eamonn was born into a large Irish Catholic family. His abuse began at the age of 12 and continued until he was 22; he was abused over one thousand times. I found the book most upsetting, not just because it contained frank descriptions of abuse but because it described how Fr Penny manipulated and betrayed the trust placed in him by the Flanagans. I have relatives living in England and through them I have personal experience of the warm and trusting welcome extended to local clergy, particularly if they are Irish.

Sexual abuse by a priest is always an abuse of power. Eamonn Flanagan describes 'the power of a piece of white plastic. It is no more than three inches long, fitting neatly behind the shirt collar. It gave Sam access to so many homes, wherever he wanted' (1995, 51). He refers to Fr Penny as Sam, and explains how Fr Penny encouraged the use of his first name to break down barriers. Eamonn acknowledges that it took him years to realise 'that his friendship line which he pushed so hard was part of his scheme to enable him to abuse me' (1995, 66). He came to realise that Fr Penny used the friendship idea 'to confuse me and it worked well' (1995, 61). In other words, he purposely created confusion by blurring the nature of the relationship. Eamonn couldn't tell whether it was a friendship relationship, a pastoral relationship or an abusive relationship, with the result that he wasn't in a position to use his own power to end the relationship. He paints a portrait of the powerful status enjoyed by Fr Penny. He was 'the greatest priest ever born. The message came out from the man himself, family, friends and parishioners' (1995, 40). Here you have evidence of the man's grandiose view of himself which is typical of a narcissist. A further indication of the man's narcissism was his 'ability to wear people down' in order to get his own way (1995, 164). Earlier I stated that narcissism exists on a continuum. Fr Penny would be placed on the high end of that continuum. Not all clergy sexual abusers have the same pathological profile as Fr Penny. As I pointed out there is no single profile that fits them all.

The author of my next text would be better known to readers: Colm O'Gorman. You may be familiar with the story of his abuse by Fr Sean Fortune in the diocese of Ferns. Colm's abuse, while no less horrific, took place over a shorter period of time, two and a half years between 1981 and 1983. Colm was fourteen when he first met Fr Fortune. He describes how 'there was nothing subtle about him; he was all force, and bluster ... He was like a whirlwind wherever he went; loud, destructive and unstoppable' (2009, 43). Perhaps the clinical terms to describe what Colm refers to here would be arrogant, dismissive and manipulative. These are all characteristics of the narcissistic personality. He further illustrates the sense of entitlement typical of narcissists as he describes Fr Fortune's visit to his family home. 'He arrived, unannounced, with the absolute expectation of an open door; that he had the God-given authority to impose himself was never in question. His collar was his pass to every home, his key to our front door' (2009, 44). Here we have a theme that recurs time and time again with child sexual abusers: a disregard for boundaries. His manner of paying a pastoral visit to a family infringed on their boundaries. He was to infringe Colm's personal boundaries in a much more serious way later on. Fr Fortune, in terms of his physical build and personality, would seem to have enjoyed a certain amount of power. Added to this was the power of his collar. Colm O'Gorman describes graphically the impact of the power on himself and his family. 'The power of that collar silenced me and blinded her (his mother); a strip of white with the might of an empire behind it' (2009, 61). There is power attached to every professional role and most professionals don't misuse that power. Someone with the developmental history of Fr Fortune and a similar personality profile is more likely to do so.

Both these short narratives which I have presented tell us much about the priest perpetrator. They illustrate very graphically how sexual abuse by any professional is always an abuse of power. I am inclined to view the whole clergy sexual abuse crisis as an abuse of power. In the first instance it is an abuse of power on the part of the abusing priest. In the second instance it is an abuse of power by those in a leadership role who failed to provide proper oversight and failed to respond adequately to the allegations when they were reported. The strategies used to cover-up such allegations were also a further abuse of power. I find myself in agreement with Fintan O Toole on this issue.

The truth is that child sexual abuse and cover-up are not primarily about religion and sex. They are about power. The bleak lessons of human history are that those who have too much power will abuse it. And those organisations will put their own interests above those of the victims' (*The Irish Times*, 17/04/2010).

In the stories narrated above we have witnessed how priest perpetrators callously put their own interests before those of the vulnerable parishioner. Sadly this pattern of abuse was often repeated by the church to whom they looked for recourse.

Celibacy and the Clerical Sexual Abuse Crisis
The question is often posed by the media as to whether celibacy is to blame for the clerical sexual abuse crisis. In profiling the priest child sexual abuser I have tried to show that the causal factors of clergy sexual abuse are to be found in the developmental history and personality profile of the abuser. Removing the obligation of celibacy from such individuals will not make them any less dangerous to children. I agree with the view expressed by Fr Thomas Doyle that 'it is much too simplistic to assume that the inability to turn to women for sexual release causes clerics to prey on children or adolescents' (2007, 150). Current research on adult sex offenders indicates that most of them are either married or were formerly married at the time they com-

mit their offences. Providing access to appropriate sexual partners will not prevent clerical sexual abuse from occurring
(Hidalgo 2007, 47). In taking this stance, I do not claim that sexual abuse by priests has nothing to do with celibacy. Celibacy can
contribute to environmental factors such as loneliness that could
lead a priest to abuse. For a priest with narcissistic tendencies,
the obligation of celibacy can lead to a sense of entitlement; that
one is entitled, so to speak, to some pleasure to make up for the
deprivations resulting from being celibate. This is an illustration
of the type of rationalisation engaged in by priest abusers to jus-
tify their behaviour.

Any objective study of celibacy for Catholic priests would
have to acknowledge that celibacy is problematic. Richard Sipe,
who has conducted extensive research on this topic, estimates
that at any one time 50% of American clergy are practising
celibacy (2003, 50). Cardinal Jose Sanchez, head of the Vatican
Congregation for the Clergy said in 1993 when confronted with
documents stating that between 45% and 50% of priests do not
practice celibacy, 'I have no reason to doubt the validity of those
figures.' (Doyle, Sipe & Wall 2006, 215). It is not my intention to
present arguments for and against celibacy. From the stance of a
social scientist I would want to point out that celibacy does raise
an issue of credibility for the church. Data such as that put forward by researchers like Richard Sipe means that no Catholic
bishop is in a position to guarantee to his faithful that, at any
given time, a substantial proportion of his clergy is in fact keeping to their celibate commitment. Meanwhile there exists an implied social contract that they are.

This raises again the question of credibility. It is for this reason that I see a connection between celibacy and the clergy sexual
abuse crisis. Church leaders seem to be turning a blind eye to the
widespread non-compliance with the celibacy requirement and
this further erodes credibility which has been already eroded by
the sexual abuse scandal. Marie Fortune, who has studied the
question of professional misconduct by clergy in all churches, is
of the opinion that the scandal of adult sexual abuse by clergy
acting in a pastoral role will be the 'next wave of the tsunami to
hit the church' (2003, 55).

Homosexuality and the Clergy Sexual Abuse Crisis

Richard Sipe estimates that over 30% of American clergy have a homosexual orientation. He acknowledges that other knowledgeable commentators put the figure higher (2003, 51). The 'Homosexuals Did It Theory' which I have already alluded to, suggests that the presence of such a high percentage of homosexuals in the priesthood is to blame for the high number of clergy who sexually abuse minors. As evidence of this they point to a high proportion of adolescent males among clergy abuse victims and a rise in the percentage of older teens (15-17) reporting abuse for the first time (John Jay Study 2004). The greater percentage of males among clergy victims may reflect opportunity rather than sexual orientation (Frawley-O'Dea & Goldner 2007, 24). While I would be willing to accept that a certain percentage of these young men being abused might themselves be gay, this does not mean that their relationship with their abuser is a gay relationship. Since the abuser's primary attraction is to minors rather than to adult males, it is inaccurate to describe this a gay relationship. Gay men are primarily attracted to adults of the same sex and not to children.

In the course of my work with priests, I have met a number who in their 30s had not reached clarity around their sexual orientation. One of the reasons for this may be the church's condemnation of homosexuality as a disorder. When one's sexual orientation is considered to be disordered by one's belief system it is not unusual to experience a delay in one's cognitive awareness of this orientation (Hidalgo 2007, 51). Some of them in pastoral care of young men would have crossed boundaries and engaged in inappropriate sexual activity. The young men in question would have been in their late teens (16 to 18). In many of these cases, I would have misgivings about diagnosing ephebophilia since their primary attraction was to adult males. In this instance, delayed psychosexual development, rather than the fact that the priest himself was gay, would have led to the crossing of boundaries. In 2003 when this controversy over homosexuality was at its height, Vatican officials consulted with a group of 'the most qualified experts on the theme.' One of the American experts in the group, Dr Martin P. Kafka, stated that while 'the great predominance of homosexual males are in no way sexual abusers, there is a subgroup at risk' (*National Catholic Reporter*, 18/04/2003). The same could equally be said of a group of heterosexuals. I think Myra Hidalgo arrives at a balanced assessment of this complex issue: 'I believe that the homosexual nature of the majority of the sexual abuse offences reported, along with a disproportionate representation of homosexuals in seminaries and convents, are critical factors related to the problem, but that homosexuality itself is not the cause' (Hidalgo 2007, 51). It would be misleading to claim that homosexuality has been the cause of the child sexual abuse by clergy; on the other hand it would be wrong to say that it is completely irrelevant. According to David Finkelhor, a recognised expert on child abuse, 'homesexuality may be connected with some of the clergy abuse in ways that need more forthright explanation and analysis' (2003, 1227).

At the end of this chapter which covered a lot of material, it might be helpful to summarise the data in the form of a series of statements:

- The ratio of child sexual abusers among Catholic clergy is comparable to other groups in the wider population
- Not all child sexual abusers are paedophiles or ephebophiles
- The majority of priest offenders are not paedophiles
- Not all child sexual abusers pose an equal threat to children
- There is no single clinical profile to describe clergy child sexual abusers
- Clergy sexual abuse has a multiplicity of causes one of which is the psychological make-up of the abusing priest
- Some clergy sexual abusers have themselves been abused in childhood
- Only a certain percentage of clergy abused in childhood (approx. 50%) go on to sexually abuse as adults
- A narcissistic clerical culture feeds the narcissistic needs of clergy sexual abusers
- All sexual abuse by clergy is an abuse of power
- Imposing the requirement of celibacy on clergy doesn't cause them to become child abusers
- The majority of men who abuse boys are not homosexual
- Some homosexual and some heterosexual clergy abuse minors

I set out writing this chapter in the hope of shedding some

light on the complex history of clergy sexual abusers and, in the process, clearing up some of the misconceptions that surround this topic. As someone who has worked professionally with clerical child abusers, I have come to appreciate all that is involved in coming to terms with this condition. Firstly, to acknowledge that one has a sexual attraction to minors as distinct from adults must be a lot to come to terms with. Following on this, one must make a commitment to leading an offending free life. Secondly, if one has engaged in offending behaviour one needs to acknowledge the full extent of that and take responsibility for it. Furthermore, if the offender is a priest, he has to accept that such behaviour has consequences, one of which is the removal of the faculties allowing him to engage in public ministry in the church. He has to come to terms with this information entering the public domain and the consequences for his circle of relationships, especially with members of his own family. Finally, he needs to address the task of putting together a new life for himself and all that this entails. These tasks are not easy. People who go through any recovery process tell us that they can never make it on their own; they need support. One of my intentions in addressing this topic is to help create that climate of support which the perpetrators and their victims so desperately need.

For reflection and conversation:
What have you learned in this chapter about priest perpetrators?
What have you learned about victims of clergy sexual abuse?
What has it been like for you to learn that priests who were trusted by the community had allegations of child sexual abuse made against them?
What is your opinion in relation to a one-strike-you're-out policy for priests guilty of child sexual abuse?
How would you like to see the church dealing with priests convicted of child sexual abuse?
What do you consider might be the value of a debate in the church about obligatory celibacy for priests?
What is your opinion regarding the non compliance by priests with the obligation of celibacy?

CHAPTER SEVEN

Spiritual Abuse: The Unhealed Wound

I take up this topic for a number of reasons. Firstly, all sexual abuse by a member of the clergy constitutes spiritual abuse. Secondly, while only a small proportion of readers may have experienced clergy sexual abuse, a large proportion has experienced spiritual abuse. This would be the case for pre-Vatican II and Vatican II Catholics more than for post-Vatican II Catholics who experienced a less authoritarian and dogmatic church. The institution which let the faithful down in its handling of the sexual abuse scandal also failed the faithful by abusing its power in a spiritual context. Both forms of abuse have been intertwined in the lives of Catholics who have lived through the crisis. Readers of this book are by this stage familiar with the different types of abusive behaviour referred to as: emotional abuse, verbal abuse, physical abuse and sexual abuse. All of these form part of the public discourse but spiritual abuse is not usually referred to in this context.

What is Spiritual Abuse?
The most concise definition of spiritual abuse I have come across is provided by Demaris S. Wehr. She describes it as 'a misuse of power in a spiritual context' (2002, 49). This definition contains a number of assumptions. It implies that those we encounter in a 'spiritual context' are people with power. The term power as used here, simply means that they have the ability to exert influence. There are lots of stories told in Ireland about the power of the priest, some humorous and some not so humorous. Anyone growing up in Ireland in the 40s, 50s and 60s was left in no doubt about the power of the local parish priest and bishop. Though many of us may not see it in this light, power is a neutral term. It can be used for good and it can be used for evil or selfish ends. Just think of the influence (power) someone like a

grandparent had over you when you were a child, which by and large was for the good. Power is used in a positive way when it promotes the well-being and freedom of the one under its influence. We can all recall words of encouragement or affirmation spoken to us in childhood and the impact they had on our fragile self-esteem. On the other hand, there are painful memories of words that made us feel shamed and second best. While we would not have seen it in this light, these words were in essence an abuse of power on the part of an adult towards a child who was vulnerable.

For many who have grown up in Ireland, some of the most significant experiences of childhood years took place in a spiritual context. Events like first communion, first confession and confirmation readily come to mind. These events touched us deeply on an emotional level and in many instances gave rise to genuine spiritual experiences. They gave us a sense of the transcendent and of our own specialness to both God and family. They contributed in some way to our developing spiritual identity which I spoke of in chapter one. Spirituality is experiential and is related to events that touch us at a soul level. I have been describing what could be called the positive side of spirituality. Spiritual abuse could be described as the shadow side of spirituality. Spirituality focuses on the higher things – peace, wisdom and love and so it can be said to have the deepest shadow of all.

Spiritual Effects of Abuse by Clergy
As a therapist I would not want to underestimate the psychological impact of sexual abuse but maybe its most profound impact is on the soul. Sexual abuse has been described as the murder of the soul. Psychoanalyst Leonard Shengold (1989) entitled his book on the effect of childhood sexual abuse *Soul Murder*. Stephen Rossetti, the American priest psychologist wrote a book about clergy sexual abusers called *Slayer of the Soul* (1990). What led these authors to choose such titles was their wish to highlight the spiritual consequences of sexual abuse. Research has found that when compared to a control group, survivors of child sexual abuse 'are more likely to feel or have felt that God was distant from them at some stage of their lives, more likely to feel anger toward God, and more likely to feel that God disapproved of

them' (Crisp 2004, 14). These are all harms inflicted on the soul.

Sexual abuse by a representative of the church one belongs to has been rightly described as a form of incest. It is a betrayal by the father of one's extended family. This is graphically conveyed in the biographical sketch of a survivor of clergy sexual abuse in the Boston archdiocese:

> I grew up in a white, very religious, poor working class, Irish Catholic family whose Catholicism mattered more than anything else. Church was family and family was Church. (Kathleen Dwyer 2007, 105).

She had placed the same trust in her abuser as she would in a member of her own family and he betrayed that trust. The Australian, Bishop Geoffrey Robinson, describes the destructive effect sexual abuse has on the very soul of the victim:

> Sexual abuse by a direct representative of that religious belief destroys the answers that the religious beliefs have given up to that point ... The link between the minister and the god can be impossible to break and it can easily seem as though the very god is the abuser. (Geoffrey Robinson 2007, 218)

In order to get some felt sense of the impact of sexual abuse on the soul of the survivor, I try to recall times when I relied on my faith to see me through a traumatic time in life and I try to imagine what would it be like if I had to face that difficulty without the support of my faith. One of the tragedies of clergy abuse is that it robs victims of the support of their faith at a time when they most need it. As we saw in chapter one, belonging to a church can be a core construct of one's sense of self, and to remove this core construct can have a profound impact (Oakley & Kinmond 2007, 10).

Spiritual Damage

In the words of David Johnson and Jeff VanVonderen spiritual abuse occurs 'when someone is treated in a way that damages them spiritually' (1991, 13). Spiritual damage would seem to occur whenever someone's sense of self or sense of connection to God is weakened, undermined or decreased. Spiritual abuse that undermines one's sense of self often occurs in the context of

shaming. Michael Nichols describes shame as 'a piercing awareness of ourselves as somehow fundamentally deficient' (1991,
30). Shaming when it occurs in a spiritual context constitutes
spiritual abuse. The most graphic illustration of the topic of spiritual abuse I have come across is in the movie *This is My Father*. It
occurs in a scene set in a church in rural County Galway during
a parish mission. The preacher (Stephen Rea) is haranguing the
men of the parish on the evils of sex and the consequences for
their 'immortal souls'. You could read the text of his sermon in a
book but the movie allows you to see its impact on the fright-
ened faces of the captive congregation. The movie illustrates two
ways in which spiritual abuse occurs. These have been highlighted in an article in *The Furrow* by Donal Dorr: 'the reduction
of spirituality and morality to legalism and the imposition of a
false conscience on very many people' (2000, 525). The preacher
of the sermon could be accused of imposing an impossible standard of behaviour on his congregation and making them feel inadequate when they cannot meet that standard. He sets them up to
feel guilty and shameful about themselves and their bodies.

In the article I have referred to, Donal Dorr, himself a moral
theologian, talks about how Catholic moral theology has tended
to over concern itself with sexual morality. He is critical of the
moral teaching which considered certain kinds of activity to be
'evil in themselves' independent of their consequences. In regard to the sixth commandment, this resulted in every sexual
thought, word or action as constituting what moral theologians
refer to as 'grave matter' and so possibly mortal sin. This was the
theology in which generations of Irish Catholics were brought
up. As I referred to in a previous chapter, it was exported from
Ireland to Australia, Canada and the United States. This misguided theology imposed a false conscience on people making it
difficult for them to distinguish between healthy and unhealthy
sexual desires and activities. Donal Dorr contends that, because
of this, most Irish Catholics are in one way or another victims of
spiritual abuse. I can lay claim to belonging to that group. When
I was growing up I would never have used this term. However, I
was aware of priests who asked intrusive questions in the confessional and I made sure to avoid them.

Spiritual abuse can take place in situations that have nothing to do with sexuality. As I said at the outset, it occurs wherever power is abused in a spiritual context. For example, it can happen when a church leader uses his/her position to control or dominate others. This can happen in parish groups and committees. Some of the most extreme forms of this abuse have taken place in religious cults. In this context it is sometimes referred to as religious abuse rather than spiritual abuse. One of the most notorious examples of such abuse occurred among the followers of Jim Jones, an American evangelist. On 18 November 1978 over 900 members of Peoples Temple died in the largest mass suicide murder in history. They had followed their spiritual leader Jim Jones to the jungles of Guyana and established a community there. The event gives rise to a lot of questions, for example, how could such a diverse group of people be convinced to commit suicide? Psychologists have come up with a number of theories to explain how this could happen. One of these is Irving Janis' theory of 'groupthink'. I referred to it in chapter four in order to explain the process that can lead a group of well-meaning individuals to make decisions that turn out to be immoral, unintelligent and dangerous.

In chapter three I related how Pope Benedict imposed restrictions on Marcial Maciel Degollado, the founder of the Legionaries of Christ. I watched a recent documentary on this group, which operated in many ways like a cult. Members were required to take a vow not to criticise the founder. During the time of his leadership of the organisation Maciel fathered several children, abused seminarians and regularly abused prescriptions drugs. The vow of silence ensured that his actions did not come to light for a considerable period of time. In the documentary former students of the seminaries he founded related stories of spiritual abuse. Seminarians were actively discouraged from leaving and when someone would leave they would quote him: 'Lost vocation, sure damnation.' This is a form of institutional spiritual abuse where the freedom of candidates to stay or leave is undermined. It runs counter to the words of St Paul who states that 'where the Spirit of the Lord is, there is freedom' (2 Cor. 3: 17).

Spiritual Abuse in the Confessional

I chose to treat of this topic because it was in the confessional that many readers may have first experienced spiritual abuse. I believe much of the spiritual damage inflicted in the confessional can be put down to a combination of two factors: i) the moral theology that informed the way priests responded to penitents, and ii) the personality of the priest-confessor. The combination of a Jansenist moral theology and an obsessive-compulsive priest could be a recipe for disaster. Jansenism took its name from Cornelius Jansen, a professor of scripture at Louvain and Bishop of Ypres who wrote a book on Augustine's theology of grace. The book was introduced into France and gave rise to a spiritual movement. Jansenist spirituality reflected the extreme Augustinian positions on grace and predestination, resulting in a pessimistic view of human nature (F. Ellen Weaver-Laporte 1993, 560). The penitent unfortunate enough to come across such a confessor was invariably put through the third degree with regard to their sexual sins. According to the manual, these were potentially mortal sins and had to be confessed fully in number and kind. No better man than the obsessive compulsive to make sure this was the case for, after all, the penitent's immortal soul was at stake. Priests like the ones I have described did not operate in secret. Their tendencies were well known to their confrères and superiors. Yet, they were allowed to carry on imposing their scrupulous conscience on vulnerable penitents. By and large no action was taken to restrict their ministry. The person with over-seeing responsibility in this matter is the religious superior or bishop. As we saw in the case of clergy child abusers, such over-seeing was frequently not carried out.

I have identified the obsessive compulsive priest as one of the likely sources of spiritual abuse in the confessional. The other person likely to abuse is the voyeuristic priest with a pruri-ent obsession with sex. Freud is credited with the maxim: 'what gets repressed, gets obsessed.' In the confessional such a person will ask intrusive questions of the penitent with regard to sexual matters and rationalise his behaviour on the grounds that all mortal sins have to be confessed, number and kind. The priest in the movie *This is My Father* fits this profile. One can see that he derives his own pleasure from his questioning of the young male penitent and ends up instructing him to break with his girlfriend because he is putting her 'immortal soul' in danger. The anger one feels watching this movie is entirely justified. One is witnessing the abuse of power in a sacred context. The examples I have presented here are for purposes of illustration and are confined to a particular time and place. I am not implying that this is everyone's experience of the sacrament of reconciliation.

Healing the Unhealed Wound

Since spiritual abuse is so widespread in the church I am amazed that Catholic theologians and church leaders have been slow to address this topic, Donal Dorr and Seán Fagan being two exceptions. I wonder is it due to the fact that a large number of Catholics have been the subjects of spiritual abuse themselves in school, seminary or from superiors that they are immune to it. It is seen as part of the clerical culture I spoke about in chapter four. This is a topic that demands urgent attention from church leaders. It is the church's unhealed wound. I agree with Jessica Rose that 'not enough attention is paid to the wounds that are inflicted within the very body itself, by individual to individual, by one church to another, or by the organisation to groups and individuals within it' (2009, 152). Hope is the ability to imagine a better future. Imagine if parishes could become places where the faithful can recount their experience with regard to spiritual abuse and receive a listening ear. Imagine if preachers were to talk about spiritual abuse and apologise to the faithful for hurts caused in the past. Imagine if the Pope were to address this topic in his weekly audience and ask for forgiveness. I am asking you to imagine a situation where the very body that caused the spiritual abuse in the first place becomes the body capable of healing this unhealed wound. It is precisely because one is willing to imagine a scenario like this that one can continue to remain a Catholic in the midst of all the scandals.

The Unhealed Wound of Sexuality

In exploring the sources of spiritual abuse I singled out the church's teaching on sexuality. Richard Sipe and Eugene Kennedy are of the view that paedophilia is not the crisis but rather a symptom of the human sexuality crisis (Richard Sipe, *National Catholic Reporter*, 10/01/2003, 9). Eugene Kennedy is of the opinion that the present sexual abuse crisis is indicative of the unhealed wound of sexuality within the Catholic church (2001, 36). The crisis has brought the existence of the unhealed wound into the open. It has also revealed that the wound remains unhealed (2001, 18).

As evidence of the unhealed wound Kennedy cites a number of factors, some related directly to the clerical sexual abuse crisis such as the extent of the abuse and the institutional attempts to conceal the scandal. Other factors relate to church teaching in the area of sexuality, for example on homosexuality, and others relate more to church discipline on matters such as celibacy and women's ordination. He stresses that it is important we avoid isolating one of the items under the assumption that if this particular issue were addressed then the sexual wound would be healed. These are only the symptoms of the unhealed wound. In fact, the expression itself is metaphorical. It attempts to describe 'our spiritual distress at the violent division of flesh and spirit that has shattered our sense of, or hopes to attain, a unified self' (Kennedy 2001, 129). That distress is experienced by all spiritual persons whether they describe themselves as Catholic or not. In order to heal this wound the church needs to recover its pastoral identity 'through which the church as mystery replies to, mediates, and heals all that is broken in human life' (2001, 184). Incidentally, it was the failure to respond out of this same sense of pastoral identity that contributed to the development of the clergy sexual abuse crisis in the first place. According to Maureen Gaffney, facing up to this scandal requires more than 'tidying up corporate governance and instituting a more transparent culture.' It requires 'the church to face up to a more profound problem – the church's own teaching on sexuality' (*The Irish Times*, 2/12/2009).

The question can be asked as to what extent the church's teaching on sexuality has contributed to the clerical sex abuse crisis. I have quoted from the writings of Eugene Kennedy and Richard Sipe in support of the view that this has been a significant contributory factor to the crisis . The Report of the Review Board set up by the American Bishops in 2002, and referred to in chapter four, expressed a contrary view: 'The problem facing the church was not caused by church doctrine, and the solution does not lie in questioning doctrine' (2004, 16 quoted in Hildago 2007, 54). Whatever position one takes on the question, a case can be made that the moral analysis of paedophile acts by Catholic theologians was deficient. These acts were perceived as unnatural distortions of the procreative purpose of sexual behaviour and not properly evaluated in terms of their social contexts and consequences for the victim (Hildago 2007, 70). One of the consequences of this was that those trained in traditional Catholic moral theology were not educated to appreciate the psychological, social and spiritual impact of sexual abuse on children.

My intention in addressing this topic was twofold. Firstly, I wanted to draw attention to the spiritual effects of sexual abuse on victims when the abuser is a clergy person. At the same time I was aware that many of the readers of this book would themselves have been the victims of spiritual abuse, especially in matters to do with sexuality. Consideration of both these topics brought a further question into the debate, namely, the role played by church teaching on sexuality in the emergence of the sexual abuse crisis for the church. This leads me to ask the question: If the church had communicated a healthier view of sexuality in its teaching and pastoral practice, would this crisis have assumed the proportions it did?

For Reflection and Conversation:
Can you relate to the concept of spiritual abuse?
What do you consider to be the spiritual effects of clergy sexual abuse?
Are there any instances/experiences in your life that you can connect to the term spiritual abuse?
How would you like to see church leaders address the issue of spiritual abuse?
Do you see any willingness on the part of church leaders to address the unhealed wound of sexuality? How could it be addressed?

CHAPTER EIGHT

Where Do We Go From Here?

In chapters four and five, as I tried to identify the causes of the crisis, I was going about interpreting it from the perspective of the past. In this chapter I take a future stance to the crisis and ask: What is the way forward? What can we learn from what has happened? When Christians set about such a task they do so from a stance of faith in God's promises. God's promise is that the desert can become fertile (Is 35: 1). God's covenantal promise to the Israelites was that God would not abandon them despite their infidelity (Deut 4: 31).

Voices are emerging from the church community today of those who can see glimmers of light in what has taken place. Bishop Geoffrey Robinson interprets the current crisis as a catalyst: 'In all its horror, sexual abuse can actually become the catalyst that produces a better church, the only force in the church powerful enough to bring about the necessary change' (2007, 232). I find it interesting that he refers to the crisis as 'the only force'. My guess is that he is only too aware of the strength of the forces resisting change. It has taken a major church scandal to overcome that resistance and challenge the *status quo*. In Bishop Robinson's view the breaking of silence by the victims became the catalyst for change. 'I must accept that, if no victims had come forward, nothing would have changed ... If a better church one day emerges from this crisis, it is they alone who must take the credit for creating it.' (2007, 225). He and others have pointed out that we owe them a debt of gratitude. In the view of Ned Prendergast 'the only proper spiritual response to the Murphy Report begins in gratitude for the gift of truth given to us all; gratitude for the gift of credibility given to victims and their families; ... gratitude for those crusts of stagnation, unresponsiveness and ecclesial deafness beginning to crack and break.' (*The Furrow*, 2010, 202). He is careful to point out that the 'proper spiritual response' begins with gratitude. However, it must not rest there, and it needs to be followed by a process of *metanoia* or conversion.

In my work as a therapist, one of the ways I have learned to evaluate a therapy session is to reflect on the level of energy present during the session. As I read the article by Ned Prendergast I was struck by the energy flowing through it. It was especially evident in the following summons addressed to his fellow Catholics:

> If you are a Catholic in the aftermath of what has been done in your name, can you deny any longer the call to find your own voice, to abandon fear and put the ounces of your weight on the line for the kingdom of God? (*The Furrow*, April 2010, 203)

The challenge he issues is threefold: i) let go of your fear; ii) take your own responsibility and iii) get up and do something. One can't embark on a process of change without first letting go. What do we as Catholics need to let go of? Ned Prendergast names it as fear. The question needs to go deeper. Fear of what? Remember what was said in chapter three about the clerical culture and the deferential attitude. As laity we need to let go of our fear of the clergy. We need to let go of some of the assumptions we've carried since childhood: they know best; they are the ones closest to God; they have the power. Now in the light of the publicity following the sexual abuse scandal we need to let go of the poor self image we have of ourselves as Catholics. As we embark on the journey ahead we may need to let go of our naïve optimism with regard to the possibility of change. Don't expect too much, warns Oliver Maloney. Those with expectations of radical change are likely to be disappointed (2010, 6).

We are in a Phase of Transition
What do we mean by the term transition? To answer this question I will draw on the work of William Bridges. As I faced my own transitions in life I have found him a reliable guide. He first studied organisations in transition and later wrote about his own personal transition following the death of his wife and his subsequent remarriage. Bridges draws a distinction between

transition and change. Change is external and concrete, for example changing a job or moving to a new house. Change happens pretty fast. Transition, on the other hand is much slower. It is the inner psychological and spiritual process that people go through in coming to terms with change (Bridges 2001, 2). All of us experience transitions as we go through the life cycle, for example the transition from adolescence to adulthood and the mid-life transition. These transitions are predictable. The transitions that cause us most trouble are the ones that come unannounced and catch us off guard, for example, the onset of a sudden illness. The examples I have given up to now are all personal transitions. However, transitions also occur at an organisational level. The clergy sexual abuse crisis is one such transition affecting the Catholic church.

According to Bridges transitions are marked by experiences of:

disorientation – one feels bewildered and lost
disengagement – one separates from what was familiar
disidentification – one's old sense of identity is disturbed
disenchantment – the old reality one accepted unthinkingly is shattered
(Bridges 2001, 62-63)

Perhaps I can best sum it all up by saying that transition creates distance from what was familiar. I treated of several of these themes in chapters one and two when I discussed identity and the crisis of loss. The part of Bridges' work I find most helpful is his division of the transition process into three phases: ending, the neutral zone and beginning again. I will now describe each of these phases and attempt to relate them to the institutional transition that the church is going through at this point in time.

The ending phase is marked by a series of losses; I identified several of these losses in chapter two. The neutral zone is where I think we are at now. Bridges compares the neutral zone to the wilderness through which Moses led the people of Israel. He makes the point that: 'Then it took 40 years, not because they were lost but because the generation that had known Egypt had to die off before they could enter the Promised Land' (1995, 37). In the context of the sexual abuse crisis his comment is very apt.

It will take several generations to work through the crisis and it will take a new generation of leaders to bring us through it. I wonder was Archbishop Martin making a similar point when he said: 'The Catholic Church in Ireland is coming out of one of the most difficult moments in its history and the light at the end of the tunnel is still a long way off.' (*The Irish Times*, 11/05/2010)

Bridges points out something else about the neutral zone which is relevant to the present crisis. It is not just meaningless waiting and confusion. It is a time when a necessary reorientation and redefinition takes place. 'It is the winter during which the spring's new growth is taking shape under the earth.' (1995, 37). This is winter time for the Catholic church. His words contain echoes of Jesus' words about the grain of wheat planted in the soil (Jn 12: 24). When an individual or an organisation is in the neutral zone, the temptation is to try and get through it as quickly as possible. Transitions take time, they cannot be rushed. For this reason church leaders rightly point out that there is no quick solution to this crisis. Wounds don't heal overnight. Restoring credibility and trust is a slow process. The changes required are systemic and an institution like the Catholic church moves slowly.

This leads me on to the third phase of the transition process: new beginnings. Beginnings involve new understanding, new attitudes, new values and new identities. Just as we resist change we can resist new beginnings. Bridges points out that we can re-press the future just as we repress the past. In other words, just as we deny the trauma of the past, we can blind ourselves to the possibility of a new future. The future is there for us 'in the form of a dimly sensed movement, a pattern that we can glimpse out of the corner of our eye' (Bridges 2001, 213). My advice to Catholics experiencing transition is to look for emerging signs of 'new life' and to support and nourish them. These are the signs of new beginnings, the fruits of the transition process.

In order to get some sense of where we are, I have applied the model of transition and described us as being in the neutral zone phase of that process. Another fruitful approach would be to explore the question: Where are we in terms of what has been achieved up to now? This question needs to be broken down into a series of sub-questions:

What has been acknowledged?
What has been learned?
What has been apologised for?
Who has apologised? Who hasn't?
Who has accepted responsibility? Who hasn't?
What has been put in place so far?

What Has Been Put in Place
Some of these questions I will address in the following chapters.
Here, I will look at what has been put in place so far. The first co-ordinated attempt to address the sexual abuse crisis by the Irish church was the publication in 1996 by the Irish Catholic Bishops' Advisory Committee of a document entitled: *Child Sexual Abuse: Framework for a Church Response.* As the title indicates this was a set of principles and guidelines detailing how dioceses and religious congregations in Ireland were to respond to allegations of child sexual abuse by clergy and religious. Structures and training were put in place to help with the implementation of the document. No audit was ever conducted to ascertain levels of compliance. As is evident from the Ferns and Murphy Reports, there was confusion among church leaders as to the document's requirements regarding the reporting of allegations to civil authorities. Certainly there was no uniform compliance with this requirement. As the Murphy Report has noted, canon law does empower episcopal conferences to declare binding norms after approval by the Holy See. The Framework Document did not have this status and was not binding on individual bishops. The former Archbishop of Dublin, Cardinal Connell, told Marie Collins that he did not feel obliged to follow the norms of the document (Mary Raftery, *The Irish Times*, 22/12/2005). The Holy See never gave it formal recognition, leaving it without legal status (Par. 3. 42). This partly explains why the document, despite its strengths, never adequately achieved its aims.

If the church in Ireland was to respond adequately to the sexual abuse crisis, several steps needed to be taken. We needed a document to outline principles and procedures for dealing with allegations. This was provided but never had the legal status required. Secondly, we needed up-to-date information with regard to the extent of the problem, the number and range of allegations, how they were being processed etc. In June 2002 the Irish Bishops commissioned Gillian Hussey, a retired judge, to conduct an audit of all dioceses and religious congregations. I recall at the time that the journalist David Quinn lauded the venture, saying it would help to restore faith in the church. When the government set up the Ferns Inquiry, this project, for whatever reason, was abandoned. Was it because of lack of co-operation or was it because the HSE was about to conduct a similar audit? We are still awaiting the publication of the findings of this audit. It is regrettable that this project it taking such a long time to complete. The data from such a study is urgently required to inform any ongoing church or state response.

In 2003 the Bishops set up a Working Group on Child Protection, chaired by Maureen Lynette. Included in their terms of reference was to 'develop a comprehensive and integrated child protection policy for the Irish Catholic church' (2005, 2). The policy was to be consistent with civil law and was to address all forms of abuse – physical, sexual and emotional abuse and neglect. In this it went further than the Framework Document which concerned itself solely with child sexual abuse. After two years of consultation, the document *Our Children, Our Church* was published jointly by The Irish Bishops' Conference, The Conference of Religious of Ireland (CORI) and The Irish Missionary Union (IMU). The Murphy Report notes that this document has not yet received formal approval from Rome and has no legal status under canon law.

In 2007 The National Board for Safeguarding Children and The National Office for Child Protection were established. A Presbyterian, Ian Elliot was appointed as its first Director. He has extensive experience working in the child protection services in Northern Ireland. In 2008 the Board published a guide to aid all parishes, schools and organisations in drawing up child protection policies entitled: *Safeguarding Children: Standards and guidance document for the Catholic Church in Ireland*. The National Office is responsible for education and training as well as conducting a national audit in relation to child protection. In order to obtain an up-to-date statement on what has been achieved, I have consulted The Second Annual Report of the NBSCCI. Introducing the Report, Ian Elliott presented his conclusions:

> Firstly, that children should be safer today within the church than they once were. Secondly, those who seek to harm children should feel much less secure.

He presented the following data to support his conclusions: 2, 356 individuals have been trained and are now acting as child safeguarding representatives in parishes across the country. He further stated that he does not have evidence of 'widespread non-compliance, but there is increased evidence of commitment to change (*The Irish Times*, 18/05/2010). The key qualification in this statement is widespread. In 2008 Ian Elliot wrote a critical report on The Management of Two Child Protection Cases in the Diocese of Cloyne, which was later published on the diocesan website. He received general acclaim for the quality of his assessment. This was taken as a sign that greater transparency had entered into the closed church culture. On the basis of the developments outlined, church leaders have put forward the claim that the landscape has changed from what it was in the period covered by the Murphy Report (1975-2004).

Response Strategies
Another way to assess how far we have come is to examine the response strategies that have been adopted to deal with the crisis. George Wilson reviewed possible response strategies and came up with the following:

- Strategy of preventive measures, e.g. guidelines, policy statements, and yearly audits
- An organisational structure strategy
- Strategies to restore the credibility of the institution
- A cultural transformation strategy

(George B. Wilson 2008, 97)

Many of the developments I outlined for the period 1996-2008 fit into the category of preventative measures. The setting up of the National Board and Office is a structural strategy. The attempts of Archbishop Martin to raise the issue of leadership responsibility could be seen as an attempt to regain some credibility. What about cultural transformation strategies? There have been numerous calls for this, notably by the chairperson of the National Board for Safeguarding Children, John Morgan: 'Until clericalism is completely behind us, we are not going to change. Clericalism is the antithesis of what the church is supposed to be about' (*Irish Times*, 18/05/2010). Earlier, I made the point that since clericalism is the product of the interaction of both parties, clergy and laity, it requires the action of both to bring about change. I hear anecdotal evidence of parish meetings where the laity are raising issues and asking questions never asked before – a sign that the culture of those gatherings is changing. There are some but less widespread reports of a similar change at meetings of the clergy. I interpret this as evidence of the new beginning phase identified by William Bridges. It doesn't mean we are out of the neutral zone. However, we haven't as yet seen the systemic changes that would indicate a change of culture. It is becoming clearer that these changes that make a difference will not emerge from Rome but will happen at local level. In this context I was encouraged to read the contribution of Dr Tony Hanna, Co-Director of the pastoral plan for the Archdiocese of Armagh. He outlined a series of local initiatives as evidence that 'the health of the church is much more robust than many commentators would have us believe.' Among these was the commissioning of over 300 lay women and men who had undergone training to take up new leadership roles within the archdiocese (*The Irish Times*, 29/06/2010).

Implications for Bishops, Priests and Laity
As I reflected further on the question: where do we go from here? I found myself distinguishing between the implications of the crisis for bishops, priests and laity. Christopher Ruddy adopted a similar approach in an address given to the Catholic Theological Society of America entitled: 'Ecclesiological Issues Behind the Sexual Abuse Crisis' (2007). Addressing the group he outlined the nature of the response called for, using three keywords: accountability for bishops, identity for priests and adulthood for the laity (2007, 121). If one followed the debate arising from the publication of the Murphy Report one would see how accurate his analysis was.

Accountability for Bishops

Ruddy identifies three dimensions of accountability with regard to bishops: accountability to the Pope, accountability to one's brother bishops and accountability to the laity. In his view these three dimensions of accountability should reinforce each other rather than compete (2007, 121). It would seem that during the papacy of John Paul II accountability to the Pope was emphasised to the detriment of the other two dimensions. There was an attempt to curtail the authority of national bishops' conferences. When the revised *Code of Canon Law* appeared in 1983, Canon 455 stated specifically that conferences could only legislate specifically in those cases in which common law prescribes it or a special mandate of the Vatican permits it.

What about a bishop's accountability to his brother bishops? The theological term for this is collegiality. A lack of collegiality contributed to the distancing of bishops from each other and to the adoption of an 'I'll do my own thing' mentality. Archbishop Martin made public reference to this when he disclosed on the *Prime Time* programme that only one fellow bishop had bothered to make contact with him following the publication of the Murphy Report. The fact that he chose to make this comment on national television might have a counterproductive impact on episcopal collegiality. The National Review Board's Report, which I have already referred to, recounts the response of one bishop to the US Conference of Catholic Bishops' five principles in 1992 where he said 'No one is going to tell me how to run my diocese' (quoted in *Origins,* 2007, 121). The tragedy is that we know this particular stance on the part of some bishops compounded greatly the sexual abuse crisis in the United States. Bishop Wilton Gregory, President of the US Conference of Catholic Bishops, in his address to the Dallas meeting in 2002, made open reference to how their good work had been completely overshadowed by the imprudent decisions of a small number of bishops during the previous 10 years. He spoke of his personal anger in relation to this (2002, 100).

In the address I have referred to, Christopher Ruddy made two suggestions that he thinks would strengthen episcopal accountability: i) a reform in the way bishops are selected and ii) developing appropriate canonical procedures for the removal of bishops who have lost their ability to lead their diocese effectively. While canon law provides for the removal of a pastor who can no longer fulfil his pastoral responsibility (Canon 1740) there is no similar regulation for bishops (Ruddy 2007, 122). This issue has received fresh urgency with questions being asked about sanctions that should be imposed on bishops who fail to follow agreed guidelines for dealing with allegations.

The culture of clericalism referred to already denies any accountability on the part of bishops to the laity of their diocese. The diocesan structure for providing for such accountability is the diocesan synod. Following on the Murphy report there have been repeated calls for a synod in the Archdiocese of Dublin. Archbishop Martin is on record that he doesn't think the conditions required for holding such a gathering are present. Enda McDonagh is of the opinion that the practice of bishops meeting alone to decide on church policy and practice has proved painfully inadequate and should be abandoned (2010, 19).

Identity and Professional Support for Priests
I spoke of Catholic identity in chapter one. Identity is a key issue for all professionals, whether religious or secular. Following on the critique of clerical culture, it is obvious that for priests identity is a core issue. It is generally agreed that Vatican II offered a meagre theology of the priesthood in contrast to its theology of the episcopacy and, to a lesser extent of the laity (Ruddy, *Origins*, 2010, 123). Questions needing to be addressed are: What is at the core of priesthood? How is the relationship between priest and bishop and priest and laity to be understood? These are all interrelated questions. One can't arrive at a proper understanding of clerical identity without a clear understanding of lay identity. In Ruddy's view, 'We need a deeper theology and spirituality of priesthood, one that can fruitfully hold together both the priest's distinctive identity and his thorough relatedness to other believers in the church' (Ruddy 2007, 123).

Related to the question of identity is the issue of power. Recent documents (*Ecclesiae al Mysterio*, Vatican 1998 and *Co-workers in the Vineyard of the Lord*, US Bishops 2005) have stressed the ontological identity of the priest and his boundary distinction from the laity. However, both are called to be 'co-workers in the vineyard of the Lord.' A key issue here will be how the priest interprets and uses his relational power. This 'permeates and shapes all other uses of power' (Chinnici 2010, 93).

A priest's identity is very much shaped by the clerical culture he inhabits. It is not just the bishops who maintained this culture, it was also supported actively or passively by a large number of priests and laity who were the beneficiaries of this culture. At different levels all bear some responsibility for the maintenance of this culture (Callaghan 2010, 350). As we have seen, this was a culture of cover-up and secrecy. In a recent article in *Studies*, Seamus Murphy SJ raises the question of clerical whistle-blowers. He observes that they appear to have been few. On the question of moral responsibility, he points out that 'Those who knew of no abuses are in the clear; those who did know and who said nothing, bear some moral responsibility.' (Murphy 2010, 312). Looking to the future, if priests want to reform the system they need to be prepared to take on the role of whistle blower when required. This would mean that they need to be prepared to report the unacceptable behaviour of fellow priests when they violate professional boundaries in relation to their pastoral role. This is an ethical requirement of other professionals and is usually specified in their codes of professional practice. Rakesh Khurana, a professor at the Harvard Business School, has documented over two thousand occupations who have a code of ethics (Chang 2006, 190). Unlike most other professionals priests are agents of the organisation they work for and don't function as independent professionals. This makes it difficult for them to set up a professional organisation with its own code of ethics. They need to search for creative ways to address this issue at different levels. The professional nature of ministry in the church requires a code of ethics (Gula 2010, 39). If such a code is to be effective it needs to be accompanied by a change in organisational culture (Gula 2010, 149). I know of some dioceses where the bishop, priests and pastoral workers have drawn up a code of good practice to govern their pastoral relations and published it on the diocesan web site. A template for a code of good practice can be found in the document drawn up by the Canadian Conference of Catholic Bishops' Ad Hoc Committee on

Responsibility in Ministry, *Responsibility in Ministry: A Statement of Commitment* (*Origins* 25, March 14, 1996, p 633,635-36).

In the wake of the clerical sexual abuse crisis there has been a greater openness to the need for all those in a leadership and pastoral role in the church to avail of professional supervision. Supervision provides a structure of accountability. If bishops and priests had a place to talk with a professional about their work issues, I am sure the crisis would not have assumed the proportions it did and much harm would have been prevented. Supervision challenges the culture of secrecy in which abuse thrives. If I know I am going to be describing my work to another professional, there is a much greater chance that I will behave appropriately. Supervision makes my work more visible and places it into a context of professional accountability. This is often referred to as the normative or ethical dimension of supervision. While there is always the danger that the supervisor could collude with the clerical culture of secrecy, I would presume that a well trained supervisor would be prepared to challenge that culture (Maun 1999, 169). I have certain misgivings about making the case for supervision solely on the basis of its normative and accountability functions. It also has a supportive function (Carroll 1996, 48). We all have a right to the professional supports we need to carry out our responsibilities. With falling numbers and increased demands on their time and skills, priests have a right to the supports they need. For someone who spends their time in a supportive role to others, the opportunity to have someone give you their undivided attention as you talk about your work can be powerfully restorative. This crisis can be a wake up call to priests to put in place the supports they need to accountably carry out their ministry in the community.

As I draw attention to the need for professional support for priests in their ministry, this is perhaps the place to address the issue of support for priests who become suspended from ministry pending investigations of an allegation. This is a complex issue that so far has not been resolved to the satisfaction of all parties. The present practice is that once the bishop is satisfied an allegation has substance, he is to suspend the priest immediately from active ministry. The bishop makes a formal announcement to this effect in the parish where the priest resides.

Nuala O'Loan, in an article in *The Irish Times* (14/03/2006), expressed some reservations about this practice. She pointed out that an allegation against a nurse, teacher, social worker or police officer would not be the subject of an immediate disclosure of the facts 'to all those with whom and for whom they work'. She articulated the legal principle that people are innocent until proved guilty, and questioned whether the church reflects this principle in the way it deals with priests who have allegations made against them. The current way of dealing with allegations has added to the vulnerability that many priests experience today. Like other professionals they are vulnerable to false allegations. The possibility of restoring someone's good name is made all the more difficult by the public nature of the allegation and the fact that a considerable time will have elapsed before an allegation has been found to be unsubstantiated. In the Catholic church, the case of Cardinal Joseph Bernardine in Chicago was perhaps the most high public profile example to date.

Adulthood for the Laity

There is a growing consensus that the resolution of the sexual abuse crisis will largely depend on the laity. They are seen as key to the emergence of a renewed church. They are the ones seen as central to changing the clerical culture that contributed to the crisis in the first place. That culture prescribed a passive role for laity marked by infantilisation and dependency. (Paul Lakeland 2003). How are the laity to escape from this oppression? They will only do so by first becoming adults. It is by promoting lay adulthood that we will overcome the sexual abuse crisis (Ruddy 2007, 123).

Various attempts have been made to describe the new role for adults in a reformed church. I have a preference for the phrase 'becoming adult'. By asking the laity to become adult we are simply asking them to become who they are; we are asking them to break out of the co-dependency that characterises addictive relationships. The term has a systemic connotation which fits with my analysis of the sexual abuse. We become adult in a system (environment) which allows us to become adult. The question then becomes: How can we create an environment that allows the laity to become adult?

Being respectfully listened to plays an important part in allowing one to become adult. It provides an experience of being understood and taken seriously. Looking back on the sexual abuse crisis, it is unfortunate that the laity, especially the victims and their families, had often to shout in order to get listened to. It reminds me of a story Bishop Desmond Tutu told: on one occasion during the apartheid years in South Africa, a white supporter of apartheid asked Bishop Tutu why blacks became so aggressive in voicing their opposition to the apartheid regime. He explained to the man that they had to shout in order to get people like him to listen to them. Often, even in the church, one does have to protest in order to get listened to. One of the most significant developments over the course of the past ten years has been that the laity are increasingly finding their voice. New laity groupings have emerged to address issues related to the crisis. Voice of the Faithful (VOTF) and We are the Church are two examples of such groupings. I hope to look more closely at these groupings in chapter ten.

What if I Stay?

In chapter one I looked at the question posed by many Catholics: do I stay or do I leave? We saw that a not insignificant group of people are choosing to leave. They do so for a variety of reasons. On the other hand, you may have decided to stay even if you are just holding on by a thread. You may be looking at the implications of staying and asking yourself: If I stay, what then? If you are a lay person and opting to stay then the question you need to ponder is this: If I stay, will I be allowed to function as an adult in my church? The answer is not yes or no. The answer is to be found in one's own personal experience. I believe that the experience of lay people over the next number of years (two or three) will be a determining factor in deciding whether to stay and in what capacity. It seems that a significant group of people are adopting a 'wait and see' stance. Whether they stay or not will depend, among other things on these three issues: whether meaningful steps have been taken by church leaders to regain credibility; whether adequate apologies have been forthcoming, and whether the laity have been allowed to function as adults at parish and diocesan level.

For Reflection and Conversation:
As you reflect on the process of transition, where do you see examples of endings, neutral zone and new beginnings?
How are you going to become more adult in the church?
How are you going to relate to church leadership?
Are you going to keep your distance and avoid conflict?
If you stay, what are you going to get involved in?
If you stay, what supports do you need?
Where do you find these supports?

CHAPTER NINE

Forgiveness: The Last Step

Forgiveness is a venerable religious idea, yet I have some misgivings introducing it in the context of the clergy sexual abuse crisis. There are several dangers in doing so. As Richard Sipe has pointed out, it can be used to gloss over the reality of abuse (Sipe 2003, 258). There is also the danger that introducing the subject too soon can lead to hasty forgiveness which in turn can undermine self-respect, respect for the moral order and for the forgiveness process itself (Jeffrie G. Murphy 2005, 33). For this reason, I have called this chapter *Forgiveness: The Last Step*.

Another reason why I hesitate to talk about forgiveness is that the term is so easily misunderstood. Here is a list of some of the most common misconceptions around forgiveness:

- Forgiveness is instantaneous
- Forgiveness is forgetting
- Forgiveness dissipates feelings of anger
- Forgiveness is appropriate in every relationship
- It is necessary to communicate with the other for forgiveness to take place
- Forgiveness is a moral obligation
- Forgiveness is a wifely duty

I expect that most readers of this book will readily identify with at least one of these misconceptions. The most effective way to correct these misconceptions is to critique them against one's lived experience. Our lived experience lets us know that we can only forgive when we are ready. Our experience tells us that not only can we not forget, but that it would be dangerous to do so. It tells us that forgiveness does not change the past but that it can change the future. Finally, it assures us that it is never too late to forgive (Kathleen Griffin 2003, 25).

What is Forgiveness?

The second strategy involves clarifying for ourselves what exactly forgiveness involves. Robert Enright and his colleagues in the University of Wisconsin have been studying forgiveness for many years. They defined it as:

> A willingness to abandon one's right to resentment, negative judgement and indifferent behaviour toward one who unjustly injured us, while fostering the undeserved qualities of compassion, generosity and even love toward him/her. (Enright 1998, 47)

I have presented this definition of forgiveness to groups I have worked with, and asked them to give me their reaction. The word most people pick out from the definition is the word *right*. It had not dawned on them before that they had a right to resentment and they were pleased to see this right acknowledged. The other part of the definition that provokes a reaction is the reference to undeserved qualities of compassion, generosity and even love. Many people equate forgiveness with letting go of resentments. While this is certainly the case, forgiveness is more than letting go. Enright holds that forgiveness has also a positive dimension: it involves some relationship element, some move towards connection. In chapter two I talked about forms of distancing that we engage in when there is conflict in a relationship. When we forgive, instead of moving away we engage in a movement towards the other. It doesn't necessarily mean that we become reconciled but we at least move towards wishing him/her well. Finally, let me draw your attention to the opening words of the definition: a willingness. This highlights the free nature of forgiveness – the offended willingly chooses to forgive. This decision to forgive signals the beginning of a process but it does not imply that the process is complete.

Forgiveness and the Clergy Sexual Abuse Crisis
The clergy sexual abuse crisis, as we have seen, embraces a wide spectrum of people, ranging from the abuser to the abused, religious leaders, the institutional church and God. Forgiveness in this context has many dimensions:

- Forgiveness of self

- Forgiveness of perpetrators (known and unknown)
- Forgiveness of leadership (at all levels)
- Forgiveness of colleagues (priests of priests, bishops of bishops)
- Forgiveness of the Institution (the diocese, religious congregation, the Vatican)
- Forgiveness of God

The range of people mentioned in this list gives one a sense of the role forgiveness has to play in the resolution of this crisis. The victims of abuse are understandably wary of forgiveness. They feel that it is letting the offender off the hook. However, as I have pointed out, while forgiveness may involve the letting go of resentments, it doesn't imply letting go of the pursuit of justice. In fact, it works best in combination with justice, truth and other prosocial actions (Worthington 2003, 38). Some victims may be afraid that forgiveness requires reconciliation with the abuser but this is far from the case. It is possible to make a decision to forgive without moving on to reconciliation. Neither does forgiveness involve the restoration of trust. That depends on the offender proving themselves worthy of some trust, which may or may not happen (Thomas & Sutton 2008, 315).

You will notice that I have placed forgiveness of self first on the list. Forgiveness of self and forgiveness of others are inextricably linked. 'We cannot forgive ourselves unless we forgive others and we cannot forgive others unless we forgive ourselves' (Rowe 1991, 266 quoted in Terry Spy 2004, 47). Some people find it easier to forgive others than to forgive themselves. Forgiveness of self is a necessary step in all healing. One can make the case that it should take priority over the forgiveness of others, since the consequences of not forgiving the self may be more severe. There is an intimate link between forgiveness of self and the resolution of feelings of shame and guilt, feelings which victims of sexual abuse often experience. This can be due to a tendency to take the blame for the abuse that has occurred (Tanghey, Boone & Dearing 2005, 144). Finally, forgiveness of self brings one a considerable distance along the road towards forgiveness of others. 'If you learn to forgive yourself, you are more than halfway there' (Griffin 2003, 23).

Institutional Forgiveness

We generally think of forgiveness in the context of relationships and so we have difficulty applying it to institutions. Just like individuals, institutions (organisations) also cause harm and they too need to apologise and seek forgiveness. Organisations are not just a collection of individuals. As communities of people, they have a life and being of their own, and so we can consider the possibility that they can forgive and be forgiven (Michael Carroll 2004, 86).

I need to point out that forgiving an organisation is a much more complex and difficult process than forgiving an individual. Organisations are more impersonal and hence are more difficult to relate to. I recall watching a television documentary a number of years back entitled *The Sun Says Sorry and Other Tales of Forgiveness*. The story that grabbed my attention was about the efforts made by the editor of *The Sun* newspaper to seek forgiveness from the parents of the victims of the Hillsborough disaster. This disaster took place at an FAI Cup semi-final in 1989 where crowd control broke down and a number of Liverpool football fans were killed. *The Sun* newspaper ran a headline the next day claiming that Liverpool fans caused the riot and were found with stones in their pockets. The people of Liverpool were so angered by this untruth that, ever since, newsagents in Liverpool have refused to sell *The Sun*. The documentary followed the attempts by the editor to apologise and seek forgiveness. In the end the process broke down. From the outset, the parents were dubious about his motives. Furthermore, by forgiving, they felt they were being disloyal to the memory of their dead children. I have told this story in some detail as I want to communicate a sense of how difficult it is to try and forgive an organisation. I also want to convey the importance of the apology when an individual or organisation is seeking forgiveness. Who gives the apology? What do they admit responsibility for? How sincere are they? These are all key variables. Keeping this in mind, one might wish to reflect again on Pope Benedict's apology. To what extent will the apology help victims, their families and all those affected by the clergy sexual abuse scandal to forgive? There is a responsibility on church leadership to do all in their power to facilitate forgiveness.

Here is a list of what they might consider:

- Acknowledge the hurt of victims
- Acknowledge injustice
- Acknowledge their failure in fiduciary care and accept responsibility
- Allow themselves to be held accountable
- Acknowledge the systemic failures that contributed to the abuse
- Repent and express remorse
- Ask for forgiveness
- Apologise on a personal and societal level
- Make proper restitution
- Promote forgiveness rituals

These suggestions are not self standing. Several of them can be addressed in the course of a single intervention, for example, a forgiveness ritual.

Learning to Apologise

One might assume that churches should be ahead of secular institutions when it comes to apologising. Sadly this has not proved to be the case. Learning to apologise has been a slow and painful process for the Irish church. I single out a key moment in that process which occurred on Sunday 29 March 1998. I was reading the *Sunday Independent* and came across the most unusual of advertisements: A full page public apology from the Congregation of Christian Brothers. The action was unprecedented. Despite some reservations about the wording, I welcomed the apology. I realised that the closed door culture of denial had been penetrated – this time from the inside. I wondered about the impact it would have on other religious leaders. Would the other dioceses and congregations follow suit? I didn't think so; they were still very much in denial.

The next public apology I recall occurred five years later on 28 January 2003. A public apology was read into the records of the High Court on behalf of Cardinal Connell. The recipient of the apology was Mervyn Rundle who was the victim of serious sexual abuse by Father Thomas Naughton. (This case was among those examined by the Murphy Report). Cardinal Connell acknowledged that Mervyn Rundle was grievously injured by the actions of Fr Naughton. He further acknowledged that before the abuse occurred, reasons for concern had emerged about the conduct of Fr Naughton and these had not been acted upon (*The Irish Times*, 29/01/2003).

This public apology was followed a few months later when Bishop Eamonn Walsh, acting as Apostolic Administrator of the Diocese of Ferns, apologised 'unreservedly' to Colm O'Gorman. He expressed regret over the trauma and hurt caused to him by virtue of his sexual abuse by the late Fr Sean Fortune between 1981 and 1983 (*The Irish Times*, 10/04/2003). These last two apologies were part of a legal settlement with the victims of abuse.

No Healing without a Full Apology
Apologies tend to take place in two contexts: interpersonal and institutional. The former is usually part of a process of reconciliation and forgiveness. The latter has more of a social function, the significance of the apology being that it is recorded in the public domain. 'It contains features that define the interpersonal apology but its purpose is for the public record' (Daryold Corbiere Winkler 2001, 33). The three examples I have given would all fit into this category.

An apology has been defined as 'a summary term for acknowledgment of harm done, assumption of responsibility for it, expression of seemingly genuine regret, sorrow for the harm one caused, and empathy for victims – each important in its own right' (Ervin Staub 2005, 449). It is clear from the definition that an apology contains several elements. It is important to have clarity around these elements as this can help us to evaluate in a particular situation the validity of an apology. The components of an apology are:

- An acknowledgment of wrongdoing
- Claiming responsibility for action(s)
- A pledge that such wrongdoing will never happen again
- An expression of regret – this lies at the heart of an apology
(Daryold Corbiere Winkler 2001, 32)

I have noticed that in recent times such apologies contain more explicit reference to regret than previously. The apology issued in the name of the Bishops' Conference following the publication of the Murphy Report being a case in point.

Survivors of clerical sexual abuse understandably question apologies offered by church leaders. One such survivor writing anonymously in *The Furrow* questioned the ability of people who have not been abused to really understand its effects. 'Do those who are apologising,' the writer asked, 'have a clue of what they are apologizing for?' (*The Furrow*, December 2000, 670). Her question is valid. Church leaders haven't always fully understood what they were apologising for. Thankfully, more recent apologies by church leaders display a growing level of awareness. This survivor's comment is a reminder to all of us to be realistic in our expectations of what an apology can achieve. Public apologies by church leaders generally have a social rather than an interpersonal function; their purpose it to regain some public credibility rather than achieve reconciliation. With regard to achieving this objective they seem to have limited value.

One of the most comprehensive apologies I have encountered was given by Rembert Weakland, the Benedictine Archbishop, who had been one of the leading figures in the American Catholic church for over twenty-five years. In May 2002 it emerged that he had paid $450,000 from archdiocesan funds to a 54 year old man with whom he had had a relationship twenty years earlier. He confessed to feeling 'remorse, contrition, shame and emptiness'. He acknowledged the hurt to his own pride: 'I am also aware much self-pity and pride remain. I must leave that pride behind.' (2002, 73). The apology was given during a prayer service in a chapel at the archdiocesan centre before a gathering of 400. I highlight this apology not just because of the sentiments expressed but because of the setting in which it took place. A ritual setting seems to be the most appropriate place for church leaders to give an apology rather than issuing press statements. Some of the apologies given by local clergy during the celebration of the Eucharist seem to have had greater impact than many of the press statements to the media.

I read an account in *The Tablet* of a recent liturgy that took place in St Stephen's Cathedral in Vienna during Holy Week. The service was led by Cardinal Christoph Schonborn,

Archbishop of Vienna. The Cardinal was invited to lead the service by a group of Catholic laity, *We Are The Church*. This group was founded in Austria after Cardinal Hans Germann Groer was accused in Holy Week 1995 of sexually abusing a minor. The motto of the service was 'God, I am furious.' The service was intended as an invitation to abuse victims to talk about their experiences and to give them an opportunity to voice their fury. The service began with Cardinal Schonborn reading out a long and dramatic admission of the church's guilt. I include the text as I consider it an honest and dignified attempt at offering an apology in a ritual setting:

> We confess that some of us exploited the trust of children and destroyed it ...
> We confess that some of us are guilty of causing the inner death of others ...
> We confess that some of us are guilty of sexual violence ...
> We confess that some of us stole the childhood of boys and girls ...
> We confess that we covered (things) up and gave false witness ...
> We confess that for some of us the church's impeccability mattered more than anything else ...
> (*The Tablet*, 10/04/2010, pp 6-7)

A similar ritual to the one described above took place at Dublin's Pro-Cathedral on Sunday 20 February 2011. It was called a service 'of lament and repentance.' In attendance were Archbishop Martin and the Cardinal Archbishop of Boston Sean O'Malley. According to one of the organisers the liturgy took its inspiration from the 'Day of Pardon' which Pope John Paul II led in St Peter's Basilica during the Millennium Year (Paddy Monaghan in *The Irish Catholic*, 24/02/2010). During the ritual both men washed the feet of a representative number of victims. Cardinal O'Malley, in his role as leader of the apostolic visitation to Dublin sent by Pope Benedict, asked for forgiveness 'on behalf of the Holy Father ... for the past failure of the church's hierarchy, here and in Rome' to respond appropriately to the victims of clergy sexual abuse (*The Irish Times*, 21/02/2011). His reference to failures 'here and in Rome' is to be welcomed in the light of Pope Benedict's Pastoral Letter which seemed to blame the local church for failures to respond to allegations. Archbishop Martin's words during the ritual showed an appreciation of the long road to forgiveness and that church leaders have to prove their credibility before expecting forgiveness from victims. Speaking during the service he made reference to the difference between apologising and asking for forgiveness. 'I can bump into someone on the street and say "Sorry". It can be meaningful or just an empty formula. When I say sorry I am in charge. When I ask forgiveness, however, I am no longer in charge, I am in the hands of others. In other words, in order to ask for forgiveness one has to first make oneself vulnerable.' According to reports, the liturgy had a profound impact on those taking part. It is the subject matter of editorial comment in both *The Irish Times* and the *New York Times*. While not all survivors will accept the apology offered, the editoral pointed out that 'gestures and rituals can be meaningful, and forgiveness has to begin somewhere' (*New York Times*, 28/02/2011).

Learning to Facilitate Forgiveness
I have just been talking about learning to apologise. This is one of the many things church leaders must learn to do if they are to facilitate forgiveness. Preaching about Christian forgiveness is not enough. They need to learn how to facilitate the process of forgiveness. I want to encourage church leaders to commit themselves to facilitating forgiveness rather than getting caught up in trying to manage the sexual abuse problem or embarking on a set of strategies to restore credibility to the church. Facilitating forgiveness is a much more gospel activity.

Church leaders frequently express a willingness to do everything in their power to facilitate healing and forgiveness. While this is admirable, they also need to acknowledge the obstacles which might block such a process. Some of these obstacles may reside within themselves. Often, unknown to themselves, they carry a wide range of hidden or competing commitments which may get in the way and block the process. Many of these I have already alluded to: their commitment to maintain the clerical culture, to protect the institution, to safeguard the assets of the institution, to protect their own self image and the *status quo*.

This concept of competing commitments which block efforts to bring about change on a personal or organisational level doesn't just apply to church leaders. For example, the teaching faculty in a college or school might want to raise the standards in the school by rewarding teachers whose work is of a high quality. However, their collective hidden or competing commitment may be to preserve the privileges of seniority. Unless they address this competing commitment, any efforts to raise the standards in the school by rewarding those teachers who perform well will be fruitless. I am indebted to Robert Kegan and Lisa Laskow Lahey for introducing me to this concept in their book *Immunity to Change: How to Overcome It and Unlock the Potential in Yourself and Your Organization* (2009). My question for church leaders, as individuals and as a group is: What are you willing to do about your hidden competing commitments? Their commitment to hold on to their power and privileges needs to be given up before meaningful change can take plalce. To be fair, church leaders already engage in many of the activities that promote forgiveness. One of the reasons the faithful remain unconvinced is that these actions have been undertaken under duress.

Phases of Forgiveness
As we explore forgiveness in the context of the clergy sexual abuse crisis it is important to be alert to the danger of pseudo-forgiveness. This could best be described as hollow forgiveness where the parties involved engage in the external act without any inner transformation. It could be the result of hasty forgiveness which I referred to earlier. In this context it can be worth remembering what we learned about the transition process: it takes time and consists of phases. The forgiveness process can also be divided into phases:

- The uncovering phase
- The decision phase
- The work phase
- The deepening phase

(Enright & Fitzgibbons 2000)

Applying these phases to the clerical sexual abuse crisis, one could look on the publication of the Ferns, Ryan and Murphy

Reports as belonging to the uncovering phase. They revealed the extent of the abuse and the subsequent cover-up. The commitment by church leaders to engage with victims and address comprehensively the causes of clerical abuse could correspond to the decision phase. The response by church leaders to the various reports, the acceptance of responsibility and offering an apology to victims, along with other steps to facilitate forgiveness, could all be seen as part of the working phase. The deepening phase will go on for several years as trust and credibility are slowly built up and changes take place that testify to the church's good intentions. I am in favour of putting the major responsibility on church leaders to make the decisions and take the steps to facilitate forgiveness. Putting that responsibility on the victims and survivors would end up being another form of abuse. In this regard it is crucial to hold to the following principles:

- Forgiveness is a choice for the injured and should never be coerced
- Forgiveness is the prerogative of the offended and therefore not obligatory (Finch 2006, 33)
- Forgiveness is by no means the first intervention in the healing process
- Forgiveness might be more difficult without an apology and restitution
- Forgiveness is not the same as reconciliation
- Healing around clerical sexual abuse embraces healing of personal hurt and systemic hurt

Forgiveness can't be Coerced
Christian churches have been accused in the past of coercing forgiveness. It goes back to the reference in the Lord's Prayer where we pray: 'And forgive us our debts, as we have forgiven those who are in debt to us' (Mt 6: 12). Christians have read this text to imply that God's forgiveness of us is contingent on our forgiveness of others. Those who have experienced abuse at the hands of others have taken this text to mean that they are obliged to forgive their abuser before they can expect forgiveness from God. Forgiveness becomes a moral obligation for them and a

source of added guilt. This kind of theology constitutes a form of spiritual abuse which I spoke about in chapter seven. As an illustration of this, I quote from the writings of a once renowned scripture scholar, preacher and writer William Barclay. In his commentary on Mt 6: 12, he asserts: 'No one is fit to pray the Lord's Prayer so long as the unforgiving spirit holds sway within his heart' (1969, 130). Thankfully modern scripture scholars such as Raymond Brown refute this interpretation, pointing out that the text in no way infers a *quid pro quo* between human and divine forgiveness. Viewing the prayer as a whole requires that all the petitions be viewed in the light of the central petition: 'Thy kingdom come.' Because God's kingdom is a reality we are empowered to forgive; there is no question of a moral obligation. In this context it is important to distinguish between human and divine forgiveness. The scriptures assure us that forgiveness is not a problem for God but it is for us humans. We struggle to forgive; the resolution of hurts is a long and painful process. We don't need churches to make forgiveness a moral obligation but we do need examples of forgiveness. Jesus is an exemplar of forgiveness. He is given credit for forgiving his persecutors. A careful reading of the text shows that he didn't actually forgive them but rather he prayed to the Father to forgive them. Humanly speaking, it seems that it was too much for him to attempt on his own and so he prayed: 'Father forgive them' (Lk 23: 34).

Systemic Injury – Systemic Forgiveness – Systemic Healing
When we explored the causes of the clergy sexual abuse crisis, we paid attention to the systemic factors. Applying the same systemic viewpoint, one can describe the injury inflicted on victims of clergy sexual abuse as systemic injury. It is the hurt felt as the result of unjust actions taken by an individual and an institution. Forgiving systemic injury brings healing to all parts of the system: the victim, the perpetrator, church leaders and the church community. Forgiving systemic injury brings healing across the generations – it can bring healing to the victims and their children. As Archbishop Desmond Tutu once remarked: 'Without forgiveness there would be no future.' To say the same thing in more positive terms: forgiveness empowers all of us to move forward into the future.

I began this chapter talking about the role of apology and went on to treat of forgiveness in the context of the clergy abuse scandal. In previous chapters I have explored at some length the underlying factors that contributed to the scandal. At the time I explained that effective treatment was dependent upon an accurate diagnosis. However, I had further reason for exploring the underlying causes of abuse and it is my conviction that understanding creates the conditions for healing and forgiveness. The more we understand about how this crisis came to be, the more prepared we are to enter the forgiveness process and receive some healing. This applies to all the victims of the crisis, those who were abused and their families, the perpetrators, church leaders, the church community and society at large. Consulting our own experience, we know that families can't survive without forgiveness. This equally applies to the family of the church. We have all been battered and bruised by the sexual abuse crisis. If we are to remain Catholic we need to embark on forgiveness.

This truth is beautifully conveyed in a song *Mercy Now* by Mary Gautier:

My church and my country could use a
little mercy now
As they sink into a poisoned pit
That's going to take forever to climb out
They carry the weight of the faithful
Who follow them down
I love my church and country, and they could use
some mercy now.

For Reflection and Conversation:
What misconceptions around forgiveness do you need to let go of?
How has understanding facilitated your forgiveness?
Can you recall an apology by a church leader that facilitated forgiveness?
What might church leaders do to facilitate your forgiveness of them?
In what ways are church leaders still blocking forgiveness?

CHAPTER TEN

Reforming the System

In chapter six I described the sexual abuse of a minor by a priest as an abuse of power. Now I wish to examine the hierarchical structure in the institutional church and how it facilitated this abuse of power by clergy and church leaders. I am drawing on the work of Paul R. Dokecki in his book *The Clergy Sexual Abuse Crisis: Reform and Renewal in the Catholic Community* (2004). He puts forward the thesis that: 'The abuse of power is at least in part a manifestation of the church's hierarchical and clerical institutional structures' (2004, 204).

All religions are hierarchies of social status and power. Power is held by the leaders who are trained, ordained and 'called' to receive it (Dokecki 2004, 150). In the Catholic tradition this group comprises the hierarchy which is made up of Pope, cardinals, bishops, priests and deacons. For many of us the term hierarchy has negative connotations. In fact, the term hierarchy means sacred rule. Thomas Groome prefers to translate the term as holy order. Ideally the function of the hierarchy is to order the variety of gifts in the church community for the good of the church's mission (Groome 2004, 199). This hierarchical structure contributes to an asymmetrical relationship between hierarchy and laity, giving rise to a power differential between them. This in turn creates the possibility where one side of the relationship, namely the hierarchy, can abuse that power.

The research sociologist Anson Shupe studied structures operating in churches which facilitated the abuse of power (*In the Name of All That's Holy: A Theory of Clergy Malfeasance*, 1995). He compared hierarchical churches where power is centralised with congregational churches. These have flat organisational structures where power resides in the local congregations and they can be said to be member-centred. In his research, Shupe found support for his hypothesis that hierarchical churches are more likely than congregational churches to promote recidivism (Dokecki 2004, 152). In other words, because the laity in congregational churches exercise a monitoring role, this lessens the likelihood of power abuses being repeated. I need to point out that Shupe is not arguing for the adoption of the congregational model. He is, however, drawing attention to a weakness in the hierarchical model. His research shows that there is a structural dimension to the clerical sexual abuse crisis.

In chapter eight, I described power in terms of the ability to influence. Sociologist Gene Burns describes power as the ability to act on one's own agenda and the 'ability, if necessary, to enforce one's will.' (1992, 7, quoted in Dokecki 2004, 137). The key word here is *ability*. Ability is intimately connected to resources. These can be internal, for example, intelligence, skills, experience, or they can be external: wealth, prestige and tragically as is frequently the case today, access to arms. In the context of clerical sexual abuse, just compare the resources of a Catholic diocese with the resources of a victim making an abuse allegation. This gives rise to a huge power differential where the more vulnerable person (the victim) was often abused by the diocese.

How an organisation uses its power is determined by its ideology. Most people associate the term ideology with a system of beliefs. Gene Burns points out that ideology is not simply a list of beliefs but rather a hierarchy of beliefs or a set of priorities (1992, 163). Like any institution, the power of the church has at different periods of history been used to further a particular ideology. Applying this to the clerical sexual abuse scandal one can ask what was the ideology, the priority of the church, during the clergy sexual abuse crisis? As we have seen in chapter four that ideology was the protection of the institution from scandal and the protection of its assets from lawsuits.

A Discredited Ideology

As part of her doctoral research Barbara Balboni interviewed twenty American bishops who were active or retired. Her questioning focused on the clerical abuse scandal during the 1970s and 1980s. Her research provides an insight into the ideology shaping the US bishops' response to clergy abuse victims during those years. The central conclusion to emerge was that the bishops considered defending the church as an organisation to be their main priority and this provided the rationale for their handling of allegations (Dokecki 2003, 130). In the Murphy Report we can gain a further insight into how this ideology impacted on Cardinal Connell, the former Archbishop of Dublin. In 2002 Cardinal Connell made the decision to allow the Gardaí access to archdiocesan files. He explained to the Commission that this decision gave rise to a severe crisis of conscience for him. He was concerned that he was 'betraying my consecration oath in rendering the files accessible to the guards.' (2009, Par 1. 33). One can speculate as to the content of the 'consecration oath' the Cardinal refers to. I wonder was it the oath of loyalty he took when he received the Cardinal's biretta from Pope John Paul II? At that moment he promised obedience to the Pope and among other things 'not to divulge what may bring harm or dishonour to Holy Church' (Available at: www.osv.com/OSV 4MeNav/Catholic Almanac/All About Cardinals. accessed 27/11/2009).

One can readily understand how this oath would create a serious crisis of conscience for him if he were later to hand over confidential files about his priests to the civil authorities. This was not a case of someone trying to avoid the law. Rather it was a case of a person of conscience torn between conflicting loyalties and conflicting advice. The 'Cardinal's Oath' that I have referred to is illustrative of the ideology and set of priorities that was meant to govern all church leaders. To the best of my knowledge the wording of that oath has not been revised. It is indicative of an ideology that by now has been discredited. If the Cardinal had the benefit of the most recent guidelines from the Congregation for the Doctrine of the Faith which recommends co-operating with civil authorities, his dilemma would not have been so acute. What we have seen in the past ten years of the crisis is the slow discrediting of an ideology which led to the abuse of power and to the abuse of victims and their families.

Models of the Church
In the view of Paul D. Dokecki one of the factors that came to light during the clergy sexual abuse crisis was the tension be-

tween the communal and institutional views of the church (2004, 162). So far in this book I have been describing the church as a human institution and drawing on the behavioural sciences to explain how it has behaved during the clergy sexual abuse crisis. The church is a unique institution; it is both divine and human (Mary Jo Bane 2004, 182). Theologians may attempt to describe the church but in its essence it is a mystery. For me the best description of the church is to be found in the Vatican II Dogmatic Constitution of the Church (*Lumen Gentium*). In its opening paragraph, it describes the church as 'a sacrament – a sign and instrument, that is, of communion with God and of the unity of the entire human race.' (Par. 1). Theologians have attempted to deepen our understanding of the church by considering different models or perspectives on the church. One of these was the American Jesuit theologian (later made cardinal) Avery Dulles. In 1974 he wrote a book, *Models of the Church*. In 1987 he published a revised edition of the book. In the book he outlines six models of the church and compares them with one another. I will focus on his comparison between the Institutional model of the church and the more communal People of God model, since these two contrasting views of the church were in conflict during the clergy sexual abuse crisis.

Most Catholics are familiar with the Institutional model since it is the one they grew up with. It focuses on the structure and governance of the institutional church. The People of God model came to prominence during the Second Vatican Council. It emphasises the communal and graced filled dimension of the church, called into being and given a mission in the world. The tension between these two models runs through the documents of Vatican II and can be said to dominate the papacy of Pope Paul VI and John Paul II. If one were to read the autobiography of Archbishop Weakland, *A Pilgrim in a Pilgrim Church*, one gets the impression that during the papacy of John Paul II the institutional model held prominence. Dulles is critical of the institutional model of the church. He acknowledges that it is still 'valid and within limits' (1987, 10) but that it 'cannot properly be taken as primary' (1987, 198). In his view the institutional elements must 'ultimately be justified by their capacity to express or strengthen the church as a community of life, witness and service' (1987, 45). He distinguishes between the church as institution and institutionalism – a view which sees the necessary institutional aspects of the church as pre-eminent. His warning against the dangers of institutionalism can be said to be prophetic in the light of the clerical sexual abuse scandal:

> Institutionalism is a deformation of the true nature of the church – a deformation that has unfortunately affected the church at certain periods of its history, and one that remains in every age a real danger to the institutional church (1987, 35).

The church is now paying the price of an over-reliance on the Institutional model during the clerical sexual abuse scandal. According to Paul R. Dokecki, the scandal has given the world 'a vivid demonstration of how a church that understands itself through the lens of the Institutional/Hierarchical model conducts its business' (2004, 196). This has left millions of Catholics all over the world sad, disillusioned and angry.

One of the 'gains' from the clergy sexual abuse crisis is that there is a growing consensus among some bishops, theologians and laity that the Institutional model of the church must be replaced (Dermot Lane 2010, 11; Enda McDonagh 2010, 118; Lakeland 2009). Is this likely to happen? For Catholics struggling to belong in the church, this is a critical question. Eugene Kennedy and Sara Charles in their book, *Authority: The Most Misunderstood Idea in America*, express an optimistic assessment. They believe that 'despite the efforts to restore hierarchy, the Pope and the bishops will eventually make a transition away from the obsolete hierarchical model into the centre of a collegial church' (1997, 201 quoted in Dokecki 2004, 148).

A Gender Perspective on the Sexual Abuse Crisis

Perhaps the most forceful critique of the hierarchical model of the church and the manner in which it responded to the sexual abuse crisis comes from those who apply a gender perspective to the crisis. They point out that the leadership who dealt with this crisis has been all male. By and large a woman's perspective has been excluded from deliberations on the crisis. This has been reflected in the failure of the hierarchical leadership to understand the gravity of child sexual abuse and to respond adequately to victims. In chapter four I compared the abusive church system with the abusive incestuous family system. We saw that in both systems there was an abuse of power. In this chapter I have described child sexual abuse as an abuse of power, the power that society accords to males (Shields 1999, 15). In traditional families there exists a power differential which leaves women and children vulnerable to abuse (Hidalgo 2007, 65). Charlene Spretnak in an article entitled, *Compromised hierarchy needs relational wisdom of women,* puts forward the view that a culture of patriarchy contributed to the clerical sexual abuse crisis. The failure to protect children from sexual abuse stemmed from 'an infrastructure of patriarchal values'. Furthermore, a patriarchal value system informed the church's response. If church leaders are to absorb the lessons of this crisis 'the wisdom of women' is desperately needed. A reformed church should involve the talents of both sexes at all levels of management.* In Ireland, before the adopting of the Framework Document in 1996, women were not part of any of the management bodies advising on the handling of clerical sexual abuse allegations.

Learnings to Emerge from the Crisis
The mission of the church is to proclaim the word of God to all nations (Lk 24: 27). It has traditionally seen itself as a teaching organisation. Teachers are first learners, and teachers of the word are first listeners to the word. If the church is to be true to its identity it must see itself as a learning organisation. In this regard it can learn much from organisational psychologists like Peter Senge who has applied this term to business and educational organisations. Senge and his colleagues describe learning in organisations as 'the continuous testing of experience, and the transformation of that experience into knowledge – accessible to the whole organisation and relevant to its core purpose' (1994, 49). In the context of the clerical sexual abuse crisis we can ask how is the church transforming the experience of the crisis into knowledge that is accessible to the whole organisation? The process, as we have seen, has been a slow one. It needs to take place at different levels in the organisation from

* Available at: http://ncronline, org/news/accountability/ compromised-hierarchy-needs-relational-wisdom-women. Accessed 5/07/10.

the local parish to diocesan synod, right up to an ecumenical council. Church leadership has to 'think outside the box' when it comes to organising the next ecumenical council. Thinking that far ahead, one might ask: What will be the composition of the groups preparing the working documents? Who will be invited to address the assembled gathering and who will be entitled to have a vote?

Saint Gregory the Great is credited with the saying: 'It is better that scandals arise than that truth be silenced.' I am sure he would welcome the truth that has emerged in the course of the sexual abuse scandal. It is clear that the major truth to emerge from the clerical abuse scandal is the extent of child sexual abuse by clergy, the impact on victims, and the abuse of power by church leaders who gave priority to the protection of the institutional church at the expense of victims and their families. A truth when reflected upon gives rise to a learning. What I will attempt to do in this section is to name some of the learnings that have emerged from the scandal. I do so not to minimise in any way the extent of the scandal, but rather to identify the lessons to be learned so that a credible programme of reform may be undertaken. In chapter eight I first posed the question: what has been learned from the crisis ? I now return to the question drawing on the material presented over the course of the book.

- Being in ministry in the church and adhering to the highest ethical standards do not always go together (Gula 2010, 46)
- Clergy sexual abuse constitutes an abuse of power and a neglect in the duty of care on the part of the abuser and those who sought to cover up the abuse
- The abuse of power by individual priests can't be separated from the hierarchical structure of the church and the culture in which they operated
- 'Culture, organisational life, and ethics are entwined like a ball of string' (Post 2006, 179)
- The institutional ideology of protecting the church from scandal has been discredited

- The culture of clericalism has been exposed for what it really

is. There are growing signs of a breakdown in the resistance to change this culture (Doyle 2007, 160)
- The Institutional model of the church has been shown to be deficient
- There is a growing openness to re-engage with the theology of Vatican II (Groome 2004, 197)
- Church leaders now realize that they must earn the trust of the laity (Butler 2006, 139)
- The laity have been awakened 'from a spiritual coma induced by clericalism' and realise 'they can be adults in church as well as in their homes' (Doyle, Sipe & Wall 2006, 289)

The Emerging Laity

One of the principles of systems theory is that when change occurs in one part of the system this causes a ripple effect in the other parts of the system. The discrediting of the bishops and the emergence of the laity could be viewed in this light. Bishop Howard J. Hubbard of the Diocese of Albany has expressed the hope that 'if there is a ray of light to emerge from this tragedy, I hope it will be an even more informed and active laity' (2003, 60). One of the benefits to emerge from the crisis is an increased readiness on the part of the laity to assume a responsibility that is theirs by virtue of their baptism. Theologian Paul Lakeland has aptly observed that 'for at least three-quarters of the church's life the best theological definition the church could offer of the layperson was "not clergy"' (2006, 9). Vatican II attempted to correct this. In the words of the *Decree on the Laity*, the Council stated that 'the laity, too, share in the priestly, prophetic, and royal office of Christ and therefore have their own role to play in the mission of the whole People of God in the church and in the world' (Par. 2). Later the *Code of Canon Law* (1983) put in place the canonical structures to effect this (see Canon 129.2). In the words of Boston College theologian Thomas Groome, 'The theology and legislation are already in place. What remains to be done is implementation' (Groome 2004, 197). Some of the forces blocking this implementation have been weakened as a result of the clerical sexual abuse crisis.

The laity were the victims of the child sexual abuse crisis. Now they are increasingly being brought in to help resolve that crisis. One example is the effort to increase laity representation on diocesan boards to advise the bishop on the handling of sexual abuse allegations. In 2002 at their meeting in Dallas, the United States bishops approved norms for dealing with allegations of sexual abuse of minors by clergy. These norms made provision for lay review boards. Before approving these norms the Vatican asked for clarification of the standing, role and functioning of such boards. The 'mixed commission' set up to address this issue stipulated that the lay members of such boards should be 'in full communion with the church.' It also stipulated that they will function as 'a confidential consultative body to the bishop' in discharging his responsibilities, thus removing any doubt as to whether such boards would have independent standing (Dokecki 2004, 184). The presence of these boards gives increased credibility to church processes for dealing with clergy abuse allegations. However, child protection agencies have expressed concern that these boards don't have independent standing. In Ireland there are lay representatives on diocesan advisory boards. According to the Second Annual Report of the National Board for Safeguarding Children in the Irish Catholic Church there are over two thousand laity now acting as child safeguarding representatives in parishes across the country (*Irish Times*, 18/05/2010).

These are examples of the laity being invited in by church leadership to help reform a system that failed to give priority to child protection. The most conspicuous sign of an emerging laity has taken the form of a laity protest against the scandal, and the formation of groups of lay people to address the issues arising out of the scandal. In many instances these movements were occasioned by a scandal in the local church. VOTF (*The Voice of the Faithful*) was formed in 2002 as a result of laity disquiet with the leadership of Cardinal Law in Boston and his handling of abuse allegations involving Fr John Geoghan and Fr Paul Shanley. *We Are The Church* was formed in Vienna in 1995 following reports of a serious allegation involving Cardinal Hans Germann Groer. Other groupings have formed for victims of clerical sexual abuse. One of the best known is SNAP (*The Survivors Network of Those Abused by Priests*). A similar process was taking place among the clergy with the establishment of the BPF (*Boston Priests' Forum*) in the summer of 2001.

Emerging Lay Groups

I don't intend to survey all the groups that have emerged from the crisis. I have chosen to focus on VOTF because its origin is well documented and its policy clearly articulated. Its emphasis on structural reform addresses many of the issues I have raised in this chapter. The first *ad hoc* convention of VOTF took place in Boston on 7 July 2002, when over four thousand people from around the United States gathered in support of a common slogan: 'Keep the faith, change the country.' Within a period of two years the organisation had over 25,000 members and over one hundred local groups known as 'affiliates' (Post 2004, 215). According to one of its founder members, James E. Post, it began as a social movement and as it developed it evolved a demo-cratic organisational structure. The group is for Catholics who wish to 'keep the faith' and are committed to reforming the church. Post identifies three principles on which this reform must be based:

> First the institution must recognise its problems and their causes, fully and accurately. Second, the institution's leader-ship must make the unambiguous commitment to transform-ing the institution through change in the structures and sys-tems that contributed to the original problem. Third, process-es of participation will be created to provide meaningful lay involvement (2006, 186).

He goes on to say that the absence of any of these elements will seriously undermine the reform process. These principles are an elaboration of the three strategic goals of VOTF. I expect that readers of this book would find little to disagree with in this statement.

The relationship between VOTF and church leadership has been marked by conflict. In September 2002 Cardinal Law pro-hibited the organisation from using church property, though he later lifted the ban. Some bishops are critical of VOTF accusing it of having 'agendas,' fostering 'dissent' and being 'disloyal' to the church (Doyle, Sipe & Ward 2006, 290). This criticism has been challenged by VOTF who claim they are more active in at-tendance and take on more ministerial and administrative roles than other Catholics (D'Antonio & Porgorelc 2007). Despite its rapid growth, the organisation remains a largely homogenous group with overrepresentations of women, Irish ancestry and Vatican II Catholics with high levels of education. According to sociologists William D'Antonio and Anthony Pogorelc, one of the most striking features of the group is the small number of Post-Vatican II Catholics (D'Antonio & Porgorelc 2007). On the positive side, the organisation in the view of James E. Post has provided a reason for thousands of Catholics to stay in the church. 'It has absorbed anger and frustration and has channeled it into a force for positive change' (2004, 226). This observation of James E Post points to a feature of Catholicism that is helping it to survive the sexual abuse crisis – Catholics are resilient and don't easily leave the church.

VOTF Ireland was established in December 2005 with a core group of people who had signed on to the VOTF International website since 2002. The website is careful to point out that it sees itself as having a 'different voice' from VOTF (USA). Apart from cultural and historical differences, the Catholic church in Ireland is not as polarized as the US church. (www.votfi.com/votfi_short_history. htm accessed 20/02/2011). The website is notable for an absence of rancour and expresses a desire to forge an even closer relationship between clergy and people, one marked by equality rather than paternalism. The website makes specific reference to the plight of clergy who have suffered from false allegations. It points to the importance of balancing the need for proper child protection with the principle of natural justice for those accused (www.votfi.com/clergy_support. htm. accessed 20/02/2010).

This point is borne out in a research study undertaken by Michelle Dillon of 'institutionally marginalised American Catholics' who choose to stay Catholic even though their Catholicism is in conflict with official church teaching (1999, 4). Many of these groups are affiliated to the *Call to Action* (CTA) movement for change in the Catholic church, established by a group of laypeople following an initiative by the US bishops in 1976. The population studied by Dillon chose to stay in the church rather than leave and 'simultaneously actualise their commitment to being Catholic and gay or lesbian, Catholic and an advocate of women's ordination or Catholic and pro-choice'

(1999, 30). Catholic, as the term indicates, embraces a broad spectrum of people, the vast majority of whom are lay and who won't easily leave the institutional church despite conflicts, scandals and theological differences of opinion. The clerical sexual abuse crisis has become a 'symbolic carrier' of larger issues that have preceded this crisis, for example issues of authority, power, church governance and Catholic teaching on sexuality (Chinnici 2010, 91). These issues will demand attention long after the crisis has abated.

Remaining A Catholic: The Journey So Far
I set out in chapter one to describe Catholic identity. This identity has roots deep in the soul (*psyche*). It can be described as a personal and group identity with strong cultural roots. I went on to examine the clergy sexual abuse crisis and found it to be multi-dimensional giving rise to issues of credibility. Next I attempted to track the development of the crisis. I chose to concentrate on a particular moment in that crisis, namely the publication of the Murphy Report. We looked at the main conclusions of that report and at the response and the impact it had on the Irish church. I critically reviewed the response of the bishops and Pope Benedict XVI to the report.

A key assumption of this study was that any attempt to respond to this crisis must be based on an in-depth analysis of the contributory causes. I argued for doing this analysis from a systemic perspective. This would allow us to examine the organisational and cultural factors that contributed to the abuse. This analysis highlighted the contribution of a clerical culture to the abuse and its cover-up. In the light of this I was especially critical of the 'bad apple' theory to account for what happened.

Having examined the origins of the crisis, I posed the question: Where do we go from here? I set out in chapter six to examine the strategic response that is required to address the crisis and looked at the implications for bishops, priests and laity. By this point the following conclusions were beginning to emerge:

- As a lay person you cannot remain in the church without engaging in some process of forgiveness
- Church leaders have a responsibility to facilitate forgiveness

for all those affected by the crisis: victims, abusers and the
faithful
- There can be no healing without a complete apology
- If you are to remain in the church, you need some assurance
  that you will be treated as an adult
- Becoming adult in the church will depend on a movement
  away from the Institutional model to the People of God
  model of church

As our study progressed we began to look at clergy sexual
abuse, and the subsequent cover up, more and more as an abuse
of power on the part of the priest abuser and the church leadership who engaged in the cover-up. We looked at the rationale
behind this abuse of power and saw that it lay in an ideology
which gave priority to the protection of the institution at the expense of the victims. At this point it was becoming obvious that
at the core of the clerical sexual abuse crisis is the abuse of
power. In chapter seven we saw that the abuse of power didn't
just happen in a sexual context but in a spiritual one as well. We
looked at the spiritual consequences of sexual abuse and of
abuse in other contexts, for example, inside and outside the confessional.

An Ongoing Crisis
The word *crisis* occurs frequently throughout the pages of this
book. While the term helped to capture some of the urgency and
seriousness of the present situation, I had certain misgivings
about using it since one normally thinks of a crisis as something
of short term duration after which we can return to life as nor-
mal (Fortune 2003, 106). As we have seen, the clerical sexual
abuse crisis does not fit that pattern. At the time of the publication of the Murphy Report, I recall an observation made by *The
Irish Times* columnist Breda O'Brien. 'The Murphy Report,' she
said, 'instead of bringing closure, is merely one chapter in an ongoing story.' During the course of the past number of months we
have been watching those chapters unfolding. In chapter eight I
used Bridge's model of transitions to look at where we are now
in the crisis. I estimated that we were still in the neutral zone and
that there were signs of new beginnings. I feel it might be help-

ful at his point if I were to highlight a number of developments which have occurred so that one might get a clearer sense of where we are now.

- The levels of denial have gradually broken down with an acknowledgment of the extent of child sexual abuse by clergy and religious
- There is a growing acknowledgment of the failure by church leaders to extend care to victims and to deal adequately with allegations
- There is a growing acknowledgement on the part of church leaders of the systemic factors that contributed to the cover-up
- Bishops and religious superiors have put child protection measures in place to lessen the possibility of a recurrence of child sexual abuse by clergy and religious
- At the highest level, namely the Vatican, there are signs that the scandal of clergy sexual abuse is being acknowledged. However, there is a marked reluctance to acknowledge the systemic factors that contributed to the cover-up
- Efforts have been made at all levels of church leadership to apologise to the victims of clergy sexual abuse
- Steps have been taken to ensure that priest perpetrators are held accountable for their actions under the provisions of both civil law and canon law
- No procedures have been put in place to hold bishops responsible for their failure to deal adequately with clergy sexual abuse allegations
- Many of the victims of clerical sexual abuse are still awaiting redress and are experiencing difficulties in getting it
- One can observe a marked difference between church leaders in their ability to face up to the consequences of this crisis and to give leadership in addressing the issues

Washing Feet
In writing a book where one is building an argument step by step there is always the temptation of trying to end up with some 'earth shattering' conclusion. For this reason I have intentionally decided to end by presenting an image or symbol which addresses what I consider to be at the core of the crisis, and because it is symbolic it has the power to break through our de-

fences, personal and institutional. I feel drawn to bring the story of Jesus into dialogue with the story of betrayal and institutional cover up that I have been exploring. I have chosen one single event from his life which I think speaks to this crisis and that is his symbolic gesture of washing the disciples' feet.

It took place at the last supper and they weren't able to appreciate the significance of what he was doing. Peter, their designated leader, resisted having his feet washed: 'Never!' said Peter, 'You shall never wash my feet.' Jesus did not argue with him. He simply told him: 'If I do not wash you, then you can have nothing in common with me' (Jn 13: 8). His footwashing was not an act of condescension on the part of Jesus, it was the announcement of a new social order – an order of mutual service rather than of social preference (Shea 1998, 152).

In this new social order there is no preferred class with special privileges. Power is to be used not as domination but as service. I see this radical and self-effacing gesture on the part of Jesus as a last attempt to educate his disciples about the nature of the mission he was about to entrust to them: they were to become 'washers of feet'. He was attempting to create a new and different culture. 'I have given you an example so that you may copy what I have done to you' (Jn 13:15).

In the context of the clerical sexual abuse scandal, 'washing feet' entails bending down to listen to victims and allowing them to tell their stories. Washing their battered and bruised feet – cleaning away the shame and pain that was inflicted on them. Taking time over the task, drying their tears as Jesus dried the feet of his disciples. It is only if church leaders undertake this task that they will come to understand, just as it was only after having his feet washed that Peter understood. One of the reasons it took church leaders so long to understand was that in the early days of the crisis a large number of them avoided meeting with victims. It took them a long time to discover their pastoral identity as 'washers of feet'. In the Liturgy of Lament and Repentance in Dublin's Pro-Cathedral which I referred to, Archbishop Martin and Cardinal Sean O'Malley invited five female and three male survivors of abuse to the altar where they knelt down and washed their feet.

The story of Jesus washing the disciples' feet is recorded in the Bible – the corporate memory of the Christian community so that it may remain true to its corporate identity. Avery Dulles captures this corporate identity in his treatment of the church as servant. I have referred earlier of the need to move from an Institutional model of the church to a People of God model. The Servant model is closely related to the People of God model.

According to this model, the church is the church when it puts itself at the service of others. In this model 'there is a shift from the categories of power to the categories of love and service' (Dulles 1987, 101). In the institutional model of church the priority was to protect the institution. The Servant model can make a difference because it brings about a paradigm shift. For me this understanding of church was conveyed in the title of a pastoral plan produced by the bishops of South Africa in the late 80s. They called it 'Community Serving Humanity.' It was a wonderful motto for a church waiting to play a constructive role in a post-apartheid South Africa.

I present these two examples of Jesus washing his disciples' feet and the Servant model of church to illustrate that there are rich sources in the Christian tradition that the Catholic church can draw on as it attempts to learn from this crisis and move forward.

In this book I have drawn extensively from the behavioural sciences in an effort to try and understand the nature of child sexual abuse by priests and religious and to explain the reasons for the inadequate response. The behavioural sciences can further serve as a resource to church leaders as they attempt to right the wrongs of the past. However, at the end of the day, church leaders will be best served by returning to the spiritual resources in their own tradition. Rollo May, one of the founders of existential psychotherapy humbly acknowledged that there is 'a great area in the transformation of personality which we do not understand, and which we can attribute only to the mysterious creativity of life' (1989, 126). All those involved in healing the wounds of this crisis need the humility to acknowledge that there is a lot we don't understand. All we can do in the aftermath is to provide conditions which facilitate healing. Ultimately the healing comes from a source beyond ourselves. According to May 'one is right in calling it the grace of God, as it is preposterous to think that the individual does it for himself or herself' (May 1989,

169). Here he resorts to religious language in order to acknowledge that no healer is in control of the healing process.

Where does this journey leave you?
Abuse, because it gives rise to secrecy, isolates the abused. The Murphy Report and other similar reports have given a voice to the abused, and broken open their prison of isolation. It is my hope that reading this book did something similar for you. Through reading a book we come to know that we are not alone. I hope it allowed you to process the impact of this crisis in a more public forum. If reading this book has achieved that for you it will have been well worth your effort and mine. The experience of reading this book will be different depending on your closeness to the pain of clerical sexual abuse and on whether you are reading the book with a group of others or on your own. Either way it will no doubt have raised issues which touch you to the core. It has not been an easy book for me to write and I don't expect it has been an easy book for you to read.

For Reflection and Conversation:
In what sense can it be claimed that the clerical sexual abuse crisis is ultimately about the abuse of power?
To what extent has a culture of patriarchy contributed to the clerical sexual abuse crisis?
Is it true to say that the ideology of protecting the institutional church has been completely discredited?
What signs do you see of a transition from an Institutional model of church to the People of God model?
What steps have been taken to assure you that the crisis is being addressed?
What action on the part of church leaders would make a difference in healing the wounds of the sexual abuse crisis?
What words spoken by the victims of the crisis have made the greatest impact on you?
What words spoken by church leaders have made the greatest impact on you?

APPENDIX

Research Summary of the Impact of the Clergy Sexual Abuse Crisis on a Group of Priests, Religious and Laity

The origin of this book lies in a course I taught on the Renewal for Ministry programme in All Hallows College after the Easter break 2010. Forty-one participants attended the course. Some were taking it as a module in the Renewal For Ministry programme and others signed up because they were interested in the topic. Their faith had been shaken by the revelations emerging from the Murphy Report and they sought out a place to process what was going on for them as committed Catholics. I recall one of them describing how she was just holding on by a thread. Many were keenly following the fall-out from the Report in the media. They sought an opportunity to have a conversation with other like-minded people about the issues raised. As the presenter of the module I welcomed the opportunity to hear the reactions of a group of Catholics consisting of clergy, religious and laity to the topics discussed. I find that one can't engage in a genuine conversation without being changed in the process, and that was happening to me as I presented the module. I sought for a way that would allow me to preserve the content of those conversations and at the same time make them accessible to a wider public. I put together a questionnaire that addressed the topics covered and distributed it to the class at the end of our final session. I gave the completed questionnaires to a colleague of mine, Dr Marjorie Fitzpatrick, who kindly agreed to collate the data using SPSS. She tabulated the responses to each question and then performed a cross tabulation comparing the responses from each of the three groups, priests, religious and laity.

Composition of the Group
The survey group consisted of 41 adults of whom 14 (34.1%) were male and 27 (65.9%) were female. I did not survey the age distribution of the group, but from observation and class records I can attest that approximately 90% were in the 50-70 age cohort.

The group was made up of several nationalities as shown in Table I:

		Percent
Irish	26	63.4
Australian	7	17.1
Canadian	1	2.4
American	3	7.3
Indian	2	4.9
	N = 39	95.1

The Americans, Canadians and Australians all had experience of the clergy sexual abuse scandal in their own countries of origin. They would not have been as familiar as those from Ireland with the details of the Murphy Report. All of the Australians were lay people.

The church status of group members is shown in Table 2:

		Percent
Priest	6	14.6
Religious	17	41.5
Lay	18	43.9
	N = 41	100

All the religious were female and the majority of the laity were female (10 out of 18).

In this regard the group is not claiming to be representative since clergy and religious are not as highly represented in the church. The relative size of the groups is large enough to make some comparisons which I will do as I report on the answers to each question.

Participants Assessment of the Crisis and the Church Response
The clergy sexual abuse crisis has been described in different ways. I asked the participants to identify how they would describe the crisis as shown in Table 3:

		Percent
A Crisis of Credibility	22	53.7
A Crisis of Loss	10	24.4
A Crisis of Faith	4	9.8
A Crisis of Belonging	2	4.9
None of the Above	1	2.4
Other	2	4.9
	N = 41	100

Several commentators have described the crisis as one of credibility rather than faith. This is borne out in Table 3 above. All three groups, priests, religious and lay, named credibility as the central issue in the crisis. More religious (6) than lay (3) experienced it as a crisis of loss and that probably reflects their experience following the publication of both the Ryan Report and the Murphy Report. In chapter two I quoted Anson Shupe who observed that credibility is a 'gift' from the lay believers and not an inherent possession of church leaders. The respondents would seem to be saying that credibility is their gift to bestow and that church leaders have lost credibility because of the clergy abuse crisis.

Participants were asked to assess the impact of the crisis. They had discussed the view of Fr Hans Küng, the Swiss theologian and former colleague of Pope Benedict's, who accused him of plunging the Catholic church into its 'worst credibility crisis since the Reformation.' 23 (56%) agreed with this assessment. The highest percentage of those expressing agreement was among the women religious.

I asked participants what they found positive about Pope Benedict's Pastoral Letter. Their comments are given in Table 4:

		Percent
That he actually wrote it	11	26.8
Acknowledgment of responsibility	8	19.5
Acknowledgment of the awfulness of abuse	4	9.8
Actually apologized	5	12.2
	N = 28	68.3

A high percentage (68.3) were able to mention something positive about the Pastoral Letter despite the fact that they were disappointed with aspects of it. This shows a maturity on the part of respondents. The fact that the letter was written was the item receiving highest appreciation. The lower ratings accorded to the other items may be due to the fact that not all of the respondents may have read the letter and so were unable to express a view on its contents. More of the laity than clergy and religious stated that they had not read the letter.

I asked participants to name what they thought was missing in the Papal Letter. Their comments are summarised in Table 5:

		Percent
Institution needs to admit it is wrong too	7	17.1
Acceptance of responsibility for failings including cover-up	5	12.2
Apologising and asking for forgiveness	5	12.2
Acknowledgment of the need for change in church governance	4	9.8
Lack of compassion / regret	4	9.8
Full awareness of the situation	3	7.3
Acknowledge sinfulness	2	4.9
A way forward	1	2.4
	N = 31	75.7

In the view of respondents the major omission in the Pastoral Letter was the failure on the part of the institution to admit is was wrong. I take institution in this instance to refer to the Vatican. The percentage of the priests who identified this at the missing element was lower than either the lay or religious. This may be due to the fact that they have a closer identification with the institution. On the other hand, a higher percentage of the priests identified the failure to acknowledge the need for change in church governance as the missing element in the letter.

Participants were asked to evaluate the significance of clerical culture in the cover-up of clergy sexual abuse allegations. Their response is outlined in Table 6:

		Percent
Little significance	1	2.4
Moderate significance	3	7.3
High significance	35	85.4
No information	2	4.8
	N = 41	99.9

Respondents show a high level of awareness with regard to the contribution made by a clerical culture to the cover-up. This may be due to the fact that they had just completed a module which explored among other things the causes of the crisis. I would be surprised if this same level of awareness existed in the general public. 17 out of 18 laity and 15 out of 17 religious considered the influence of clerical culture to be highly significant, while 3 out of 6 of the priests considered this to be the case. As priests they would be more immersed in the culture and more inclined to downplay its significance.

One of the questions explored in the module was the level of responsibility borne by the laity in the maintenance of the clerical culture. Participants were asked whether they considered it fair to hold the laity responsible The majority 46.3% replied in the affirmative, with 14.6% not sure. A comparison of laity with religious showed that the majority of the laity were in agreement and a majority of religious disagreed. I was surprised to find that a majority of the laity were willing to hold themselves responsible for supporting a clerical culture. I thought they might resist this suggestion.

When asked how satisfied they were with the response of church leaders to the Murphy Report participants expressed the following levels of satisfaction. Table 7:

		Percent
Less than satisfied	20	48.8
Moderately satisfied	17	41.5
Very satisfied	1	2.4
Unsure	1	2.4
	N = 39	95.1

Only one respondent expressed being very satisfied with the response of church leaders. This is significant coming from a group with such a high percentage of priests and religious (56.1). The dissatisfaction embraces all sectors of the church community. The lowest percentage of moderately satisfied was among the laity, indicating a higher level of dissatisfaction in that group.

I have made the point that this group of 41 can in no way be considered as representative of the general population. In the light of this, I compared levels of satisfaction with the church leaders' response with the findings of *The Irish Times* Ipsos/Mrbi Poll taken in June 2010, a month later than my survey. There the satisfaction levels are much lower. 11% were of the opinion that the church has responded adequately and 83% considered the response to be inadequate (*Irish Times* 14/06/2010).

Following the publication of the Murphy Report, the question arose as to whether those bishops criticised in the report should accept responsibility for their failures and offer their resignation. Participants were asked their views on this matter. 48.8% said they should resign. Allowing for the fact that the issue was contentious, it is not surprising that a significant number said they were unsure (26.8%). The highest percentage of those in favour of resignations was among the laity. While participants were not surveyed on their views about whether Cardinal Seán Brady should resign, it is interesting to compare *The Irish Times* Ipsos/MRBI Poll on this question with our survey group, in terms of those who expressed themselves as unsure or don't know. As indicated above 26.8% said they were unsure, while in the Ipsos/MRBI poll 9% responded in the 'don't know' category. Does this mean that the public at large are more black and white in their assessment of this issue or does it imply that a group with a greater composition of priests, religious and laity are more reluctant to make a judgement on the issue?

The general question of accountability for church leaders who failed to follow correct procedures in handling clergy abuse allegations was discussed in the module. Participants were asked whether they thought these should resign. 63.4% said they should resign.

There was equal support across all groups of priests, religious and laity for holding leadership accountable.

Looking to the Future
Since the title of the module being taught was 'Remaining A Catholic After the Murphy Report,' it was appropriate to ask participants how hopeful they were about the ability of present church leadership to bring about the necessary reforms. Their response is outlined in Table 8:

		Percent
Less than hopeful	17	41.5
Moderately hopeful	22	53.7
Very hopeful	1	2.4
	N = 39	97.6

Similar to Table 7, only one of the respondents expressed themselves as very hopeful about the ability of present church leadership to bring about the necessary reforms. A significant number expressed themselves as moderately hopeful. This group comprises a significant number of priests and religious (15 out of 22). This is in line with their higher level of satisfaction with church leadership response to the crisis. The majority of laity expressed themselves as less than hopeful (11 out of 18). Again this corresponds to their lower level of satisfaction with the leadership response. Perhaps the significant factor to note is that there is hope to build on and it exists at moderate levels in all groups. I wonder whether the level of hopefulness expressed in the group is reflective of the Catholic population generally? Some commentators would be more pessimistic about the ability of present leadership to effect change. Sean Ruth, who has acted in a consultative and training role with many church groups and leadership is of the opinion that: 'With the best will in the world, male clerics are never going to be clear enough in their thinking to provide the necessary leadership for a diverse church' (2010, 108).

Participants were asked to suggest changes that would make a difference to the way the church functions. The following are the most frequently cited suggestions: Table 9:

		Percent
Laity to have a greater role	12	29.3
Involve women more / ordination of women	10	24.4
Make changes to authority / leadership	8	19.5
Express forgiveness	3	7.3
More dialogue between laity and clergy	2	4.9
Allow parish councils to have decision making powers	2	4.9
	N = 37	90.3

All commentators on the crisis stress the importance of the laity in reforming the church. Not surprisingly, it is mentioned by the highest percentage of respondents. What is significant is that not one of the priests group mentioned it. The change receiving greatest support from this group was giving greater decision powers to parish councils, a body they would be intimately involved with. The two changes receiving the highest support both refer to granting greater involvement to laity and to women. This is an acknowledgment that these groups are denied this at present. The suggestions put forward by the survey group reflect the analysis made by a wide range of commentators on the crisis. In the view of theologian Paul Lakeland we need to foster lay adulthood to overcome the sexual abuse crisis (2003).

In keeping with the focus of the module taught, participants were asked if they considered leaving the church because of the child sexual abuse scandal. Five responded in the affirmative and two of these were religious. The ratio (2 out of 17) is too small to allow any generalisation. However, it does give an insight into the profound impact of the crisis on clergy and religious, leading some to consider changing a life long commitment. Participants were further asked if they knew of anyone who had left the church because of the scandal. 13 (31.7%) replied in the affirmative. This level of response would seem to indicate that a considerable number of the faithful have left the Catholic church as a result of the clergy abuse scandal. A comparison with the number of people who have used the *Count Me Out* website to formally leave the church (7,000 as of 10/02/2010) would not seem to support this view.

The participants, who all describe themselves as Catholic, were asked to name what keeps them in the church at this time. The responses are codified in Table 10:

		Percent
My relationship with God	18	43.9
Loyalty to the church	8	19.5
My role in passing on the faith to children	6	14.6
Going back to the real gospel message	5	12.2
My need for community	2	4.9
Sacraments/liturgy	1	2.4
	N = 40	97.5

It is significant that such a high percentage (43.9) mentioned a personal relationship with God as the significant factor that keeps them in the church. 11 out of 17 who mentioned this factor were religious. The fact that this factor received such strong support is perhaps indicative of what people are looking for from the church, namely, spiritual support. Seven out of the eight who mentioned loyalty to the church were either priests or religious. This is not surprising since in the eyes of many they are considered to be 'married' to the church. The six respondents who mentioned their role in passing on the faith to children were all laity. It is widely accepted that children keep lay persons in their marriage and I wonder if children are not the reason why many decide to stay in the church at a time of crisis? Ironically, it is the abuse of children that may cause them to leave the church.

Discussion
My overall impression as I study this data is that the clergy abuse crisis has profoundly impacted on this group of people and they are taking it seriously. These are people who have made their home in the church and their sense of belonging and attachment has been shaken. A high percentage (53.7%) referred to the crisis as one of credibility. As we all know when credibility becomes an issue in a relationship that relationship becomes threatened. I was satisfied to learn that over 80% of the group found the module 'highly supportive'. This confirms for me the value of providing Catholics with an opportunity where they

can have conversations about faith issues that are of concern to them and experience group support.

Public attention on the impact of the crisis has largely been focused on the victims of clergy abuse and on the laity. The data gave an insight into an almost forgotten group in this crisis, namely, women religious. For most of the time they remain in the wings, so to speak. Over a third of them (6 out of 17) described the crisis as a crisis of loss. I commented that this reflects their experience. Most of these are elderly religious and when they entered religious life the value of the currency was high, now it has been devalued in their own eyes and in the eyes of the public. In their old age they are left with a devalued currency. I use this metaphor to convey a sense of the depth of loss they are experiencing. It was also significant that two of this group indicated that they considered leaving the church because of the clergy sexual abuse scandal. I can only guess that it gave rise to issues of integrity for them. The fact is the number acknowledging this personal crisis was small (2), but it constitutes over 10% of the group and should not blind us to the significant number of religious who may be experiencing a similar crisis. Obviously, whether to remain in the Catholic church is not just an issue confined to the laity. I would like to see further more in-depth studies with regard to the impact of the crisis on this group of people who have played such an important role in the Irish church.

The composition of the group provided an opportunity to compare three categories of church members in terms of their assessment of the crisis. Not surprisingly the laity were less satisfied than the other two groups with the response of church leadership. They were also less hopeful about the ability of the same leadership to bring about the necessary reforms. There were indications that the priests as a group identified more with the clerical culture and church leadership. For example, a greater percentage of religious and laity were more willing to acknowledge the contribution of clerical culture to the crisis.

In the light of these observations, I think it is accurate to conclude that there are significant differences in the way that the crisis impacted on priests, religious and laity. This is an issue I would like to see explored in greater depth.

Limitations of the Study

The obvious limitation of the study is the small size of the group which could not be taken as representative. For this reason one has to be very careful about applying conclusions to the general population. I have no doubt that the study was worth undertaking, again due to the composition of the group. It was a unique opportunity to survey a group with representatives from priests, religious and laity who had taken part in a joint programme designed to raise awareness about the topic under investigation. All members of the group could be considered to have a good level of education. They critically assessed the role of church leadership in the crisis from the perspective of informed and committed insiders. For this reason alone, I think their views are worth recording and listening to. The study gives one a glimpse into the impact of the crisis on such a group. I have highlighted some of the key findings and hopefully have given some indications as to the direction of further more indepth research in this area.

I presented the findings of my research in a paper given at a conference entitled *Broken Faith: Revisioning the Church in Ireland*, at the Milltown Institute, Dublin, 6-9 April 2011.

Acknowledgements

The poet Brendan Kennelly after he came through a serious illness wrote a poem which he entitled *Begin*:

> Begin again to the summoning birds,
> to the sight of light in the window,
> begin to the roar of morning traffic
> all along Pembroke Road.

Writing this book has been part of my Begin Again experience following a life threatening illness. Discovering that I had the energy to address this topic let me know that I was truly on the road to recovery. I wish to thank Dr Gerry McEntee and his medical team, along with the nursing and medical staff at the Mater and Lourdes hospitals for their professional care to me at that time. Most especially I thank my wife Bernadette McCarrick who was the main source of my emotional support along with my family, colleagues, students and friends. She has also acted as proof reader and editor during the drafting stages of this text as well as taking on all the extra house keeping duties from which I generously dispensed myself.

I wish to express my appreciation to Donna Doherty, a former student of mine and now working with Veritas Publications, who helped with the initial drafts of this text. I consider myself fortunate to have been able to draw on the advice of former students, friends and colleagues in the writing of the book. Among these I mention Ann Caufield, Professor Jim Malone and Dr Tony Draper. Collette Stevenson formerly directed the Child Protection Office at CORI and now works with the National Board for Safeguarding Children in the Catholic Church. Collette first recruited me into working in this area in the mid 1990s. I have learned much from her deep humanity which always puts the person before institutions and regulations.

Prior to publication I submitted a draft of the book to three people who in different ways have their own unique perspective on the clergy sexual abuse crisis: Baroness Nuala O'Loan, who was Police Ombudsman in Northern Ireland from 1997 to 2007; Bernadette Fahy, co-founder of the Aislinn Centre, working with survivors of institutional abuse; and Marie Collins, a survivor of clergy sexual abuse in the Dublin Archdiocese. I wish to put on record my deep gratitude for their willingness to give me feedback on my contribution to this topic.

In 1999 I spent a year on a post-doctoral fellowship at the Southdown Institute in Toronto, a residential centre specialising in the treatment of clergy and religious with mental health issues. I wish to express my gratitude to the Director at the time Dr Donna Markham and to my colleagues on the clinical staff who impressed me greatly with their dedication to promoting healing for a wounded population of church workers. Since 1993 I have been a staff member at All Hallows College. I consider myself fortunate to be working with such a warm and dedicated group of people who in various ways have been supportive of this book. Mary Ann Maxwell and Bernadette Geraghty facilitated me in teaching a course based on material from the book on the Renewal for Ministry Programme. I wish to thank the students from that programme who took part in the research. Dr Marjorie Fitzpatrick proved an invaluable help in the computer processing of the data. I would not have had the time to devote to this book if it had not been for the generosity of Moya Curran who carried out her duties as Director of the Masters Programme in Leadership and Pastoral Care during my illness and for several years subsequently.

Finally, I wish to express my gratitude to Seán O Boyle of Columba Press for offering a home to this book. I have come to appreciate the value of having access to an independent publisher when it comes to writing on a controversial topic such as clergy sexual abuse. His readiness to take the book on board contributed greatly to the integrity of the project.

References

Allen, John. 2009. *The Future Church: how ten trends are revolutionizing the church*. New York: Doubleday.

American Psychiatric Association. 1994. *Diagnostic Criteria from DSM-IV*. Washington DC: American Psychiaric Association.

Bane, Mary Jo. 2004. "Voice and Loyalty in the Church: The People of God, Politics, and Management" in Common Calling: *The Laity & Governance of the Catholic Church* (Pope, Stephen J. ed.). Washington, DC: Georgetown University Press.

Barclay, William. 1969. *The Gospel of Matthew*. Philadelphia: Westminster Press.

Bartunek, Jean M., Hinsdale, Mary Ann, & Keenan, James F. 2006 (eds). *Church Ethics and Its Organizational Context: Learning from the Sex Abuse Scandal in the Catholic Church*. Lanham, MD: Rowman & Littlefield Publishers.

Beier, Klaus M. 2010. 'Why does Child sex-abuse happen?' *The Tablet* 13/03/2010.

Bradley, Denis. 2010. 'Can the Church Reform?' *Doctrine & Life*. Vol 60, No 6, July/August 2010, p 2-9.

Brady, Conor. 2009. 'A Cradle Catholic' in *What Being Catholic Means to Me* (Littleton John & Maher Eamon eds) Dublin: Columba Press.

Bridges, William. 1995. *Managing Transitions: Making the Most Of Change*. London: Nicholas Brealey Publishing.

Bridges, William. 2001. *The Way of Transition: Embracing Life's Most Difficult Moments*. Cambridge, Mass: Perseus Publishing.

Burns, Gene. 1992. *The Frontiers of Catholicism: The Politics of Ideology in a Liberal World*. Berkeley: University of California Press.

Butler, Francis J. 2006. 'A Professional Code of Ethics Reflecting the Nature of a Christian Vocation and an Understanding of Leadership in the Church' in *Church Ethics and Its Organizational Context* (Bartunek *et al* eds). Lanhan, MD: Rowan & Littlefield Publishers.

Callaghan, Brendan. 2010. 'On scandal and scandals: the psychology of clerical Paedophilia' in *Studies* Vol 99, No 395, p 343-356.

Carroll, James. 2003. *Toward A New Catholic Church*. New York: Mariner Books.

Carroll, James. 2009. *Practising Catholic: An exhilarating journey for all those who wish to reclaim their faith*. New York: Mariner Books.

Carroll, Michael. 1996. *Counselling Supervision: Theory, Skills and Practice*. London: SAGE.

Carroll, Michael. 2004. 'Organizations & Forgiveness: the Challenge' in *Forgiveness and the Healing Process: A Central Therapeutic Concern*. (Ransely, Cynthia & Spy, Terri, eds) Hove, East Sussex: Brunner-Routledge.

Chang, Patricia M. Y. 2006. 'An Ethical Church Culture' in *Church Ethics and Its Organizational Context*. (Bartunek, Hinsdale & Keenan eds). Lanham: Md: Rowan & Littlefield.

Chinnici, Joseph P. 2010. *When Values Collide: The Catholic Church, Sexual Abuse, And the Challenges of Leadership*. Maryknoll, New York: Orbis Books.

Coleridge, Archbishop Mark. 2010. 'The Sex Abuse Crisis and the Culture of the Church' in *Origins*, Vol 40, No 4. 3/06/2010, pp 49-54.

Collins, Marie. 2010. 'Journey to Loss: Living the Murphy Report' in *The Dublin/Murphy Report: A Watershed for Irish Catholicism?* (Littleton, John & Maher, Eamon, eds) Dublin: Columba Press.

Commission of Investigation Report into the Diocese of Ferns (The Ferns Report). 2005. Dublin: The Stationary Office.

Commission of Investigation Report into the Archdiocese of Dublin (Murphy Report). 2009. Dublin: The Stationary Office.

Comte-Sponville, Andre. 2007. *The Book of Atheist Spirituality: An Elegant Argument for Spirituality Without God*. London: Bantam Books.

Conway, Eamonn. 2002. 'Touching Our Wounds" in *The Furrow*, May 2002.

Cozzens, Donald. 2002. *Sacred Silence: Denial and the Crisis in the Church*. Collegeville, MN: The Liturgical Press.

Cozzens, Donald. 2010. 'Culture that Corrodes' in *The Tablet* 5/12/2010.

Crisp, Beth R. 2004. 'Spiritual Direction and Survivors of Sexual Abuse' in *The Way*, 43/2, April 2004, pp 7-17.

Daly, Pádraig J. 2010. *Afterlife*. Dublin: Dedalus Press.

D'Antonio, William & Pogorelc, Anthony. 2007. *Voices of the Faithful: Loyal Catholics Striving for Change*. New York: The Crossroad Publishing Co.

D'Antonio, William, James D. Davidson, Dean R. Hoge and Mary L. Gautier. 2007. *American Catholics Today: New Realities of their Faith and their Church*. Lanham, MD: Sheed & Ward

Dillon, Michele. 1999. *Catholic Identity: Balancing Reason, Faith, and Power*. New York: Cambridge University Press.

Dokecki, Paul R. 2004. *The Clergy Sexual Abuse Crisis: Reform and Renewal in the Catholic Community*. Washington, DC: Georgetown University Press.

Dorr, Donal. 2000. 'Sexual Abuse and Spiritual Abuse' in *The Furrow*, October 2000. pp 522-531.

Dowling, Teresa. 2000. 'Young Catholic Adults in Ireland' in *Young Catholics at the New Millennium* (Fulton *et al* eds.). Dublin: University College Dublin Press.

Doyle, Thomas P., Sipe, A. W. R., & Wall Patrick J. 2006. *Sex, Priests, and Secret Codes: The Catholic Church's 2,000-Year Paper Trail of Sexual Abuse.* Los Angles: Volt Press.

Doyle, Thomas. 2007. 'Clericalism and Catholic Clergy Sexual Abuse' in *Predatory Priests, Silenced Victims: The Sexual Abuse Crisis and the Catholic Church.* (Frawley-O'Dea Mary Gail & Goldner, Virginia, eds) Mahwah, New Jersey: The Analytic Press.

Duckro, Paul & Marc Falkenhain. 2000. 'Narcissism Sets Stage for Clergy Sexual Abuse' in *Human Development*, Vol 21, No 3 Fall 2005. pp 24-28.

Dulles, Avery. 1987. *Models of the Church* (Second ed). Dublin: Gill & Macmillan.

Dwyer, Kathleen M. 2007. 'Surviving Is What I Know; Living Is What I Am Learning' in *Predatory Priests, Silenced Victims* (Frawley-O'Dea & Goldner eds). Mahwah: The Analytic Press.

Egan, Gerard. 1994. *Working the Shadow Side: A Guide to Positive Behind-The-Scenes Management.* San Francisco: Jossey-Bass.

Egan, Kevin. 2006. 'Confronting Institutional Denial: Two Recent Reports on the Sexual Abuse Crises' in *Doctrine and Life*, Vol 56, No 2, February 2006, 15-29.

Enright, Robert D & Johanna North (eds). 1998. *Exploring Forgiveness.* Wisconsin: The University of Winconsin Press.

Enright, Robert D. & Fitzgibbon, Richard P. 2000. *Helping Clients Forgive: An Empirical Guide for Resolving Anger and Restoring Hope.* Washington DC: American Psychological Association.

Erlandson, Gregory & Matthew Bunson. 2010. *Pope Benedict XVI and the Sexual Abuse Crisis.* Huntington IN: Our Sunday Visitor.

Ferder, Fran & Heagle, John. 2002. 'Clerical Sexual Abuse: Exploring Deeper Issues' in *National Catholic Reporter*, 10/05/2002.

Finch, Raymond J. 2006. 'Trauma and Forgiveness: A Spiritual Journey' in *Journal of Spirituality in Mental Health*, Vol 9 (2) 2006, 27-42.

Finkelhor, David. 2003. 'The legacy of the clergy sexual abuse scandal' in *Child Abuse & Neglect* 27, 1225-1229.

Flanagan, Eamonn. 1995. *Father and Me: A Story of Sexual Abuse at the Hands of a Catholic Priest.* North Blackburn, Victoria: HarperCollins

Flannery, Tony (ed). 2009. *Responding to the Ryan Report.* Dublin: Columba Press.

Fortune, Marie M. & Longwood, W. Merle (eds). 2003. *Sexual Abuse in the Catholic Church: Trusting the Clergy?* Binghamton, New York: The Haworth Pastoral Press.

Fortune, Marie M. 2003. 'Conclusion' in *Sexual Abuse in the Catholic Church: Trusting the Clergy?* (Fortune & Longwooed eds) Binghamton, New York: The Haworth Pastoral Press.

Frawley-O'Dea, Mary & Goldner, Virginia (eds). 2007. *Predatory Priests, Silenced Victims: The Sexual Abuse Crisis and the Catholic Church.* Mahwah, NJ: The Analytic Press.

Friedman, Edwin. 1985. *Generation to Generation: Leadership in Church and Synagogue.* New York: Guilford Press.

Fulton, John *et al.* 2000. *Young Catholics at the New Millennium: The Religion and Morality of Young Adults in Western Countries.* Dublin: University College Dublin Press.

Gilbert, Roberta M. 1992. *Extraordinary Relationships: A New Way of Thinking About Human Interactions.* New York: John Wiley.

Goode, Helen, McGee Hannah & Ciaran O'Boyle. 2003. *Time to Listen: Confronting Child Sexual Abuse by Catholic Clergy in Ireland.* Dublin: The Liffey Press.

Grant, Robert. 1994. *Healing the Soul of the Church: Ministers Facing their own Childhood Abuse and Trauma.* Burlingame, CA: Published Privately.

Greeley, Andrew. 2004. *The Catholic Revolution: New Wine, Old Wineskins, and the Second Vatican Council.* Berkely, CA: University of California Press.

Gregory, Bishop Wilton. 2002. Presidential Address Opening Dallas Meeting. *Origins,* Vol 32, No 7, 27/06/2002. pp 98-117.

Griffin, Kathleen. 2003. The Forgiveness Formula: *Why Letting Go is Good for You and How to Make It Happen.* London: Simon & Schuster.

Groome, Thomas E. 2002. *What Makes Us Catholic: Eight Gifts for Life.* New York: HarperOne

Groome, Thomas E. 2004. 'Good Governance, the Domestic Church and Religious Education' in *Common Calling: The Laity & Governance of the Catholic Church.* (Pope, Stephen J. ed) Washington DC: Georgetown University Press.

Gula, Richard. 2010. *Just Ministry.* New York: Paulist Press.

Hannon, Patrick. 2010. 'Collective Responsibility' in *The Furrow,* June 2010, pp 331-338.

Hidalgo, Myra L. 2007. *Sexual Abuse and the Culture of Catholicism.* New York: The Haworth Maltreatment & Trauma Press.

Hoge, Dean R. *et al* (eds). 2001. *Young Adult Catholics: Religion in the Culture of Choice.* Notre Dame, IN: University of Notre Dame Press.

Hubbard, Howard J. 2003. 'Response to Donald B. Couzzens' in *Sexual Abuse in the Catholic Church: Trusting the Clergy?* (Fortune, Marie M & Longwood, W. Merle eds) Binghampton, NJ: The Haworth Pastoral Press.

Irish Bishops' Conference *et al.* 1996. *Child Sexual Abuse: Framework for a Church Response – Report of the Irish Catholic Bishops' Advisory Committee on Child Sexual Abuse by Priests and Religious.* Dublin: Veritas.

Irish Bishops' Conference *et al.* 2005. *Our Children, Our Church: Child Protection Policies and Procedures for the Catholic Church in Ireland.* Dublin: Veritas.

Israely, Jeff & Chua-Eoan, Howard. 2010. 'Why Being Pope Means Never Having to Say You're Sorry' in *Time* Magazine, 7/06/2010.

John Jay College of Criminal Justice (2004). *The Nature and Scope of the Problem of Sexual Abuse of Minors by Catholic Priests and Deacons in the United States: A Research Study Conducted by the John Jay College of Criminal Justice.* Uscch.org (United States Conference of Catholic Bishops website).

Johnson, David & Van Vonderen, Jeff. 1991. *The Subtle Power of Spiritual Abuse.* Minneapolis, MN: Bethany House Publications.

Keenan, Marie. 2002. 'Sexual Abuse: the Heart of the Matter' in *The Furrow*, November 2002.

Keenan, Marie. 2009. '"Them and Us': The Clergy Child Sexual Offender as 'Other'" in *Responding to the Ryan Report* (Flannery, Tony, ed) Dublin: Columba Press.

Keenan, Marie. 2010. 'An Organizational Cultural Perspective on Child Sexual Abuse in the Catholic Church' in *Doctrine & Life*, Vol, 60, No 8, October 2010.

Kegan, Robert and Laskow Lahey, Lisa. 2009. *Immunity to Change: How to Overcome It and Unlock the Potential in Yourself and Your Organization.*

Kennedy, Eugene. 2001. *The Unhealded Wound: The Church and Human Sexuality.* New York: St Martin's Press.

Kennedy, Eugene and Charles, S. C. 1997. *Authority: The most misunderstood idea in America.* New York: Free Press.

Kenny, Colum. 2010. 'Sacred, Heart, Sacred Mind: The Challenge of Conviction in the Catholic Church' in *The Dublin/Murphy Report: A Watershed for Irish Catholicism?* (Littleton & Maher eds). Dublin: Columba Press.

Kochansky, Gerald E. & Murray Cohen 2007. 'Priests who Sexualize Minors: Psychodynamic, Characterological, and Clerical Considerations' in *Predatory Priests, Silenced Victims* (Frawley-O'Dea & Goldner eds.). Mahwah, NJ: The Analytic Press.

Lakeland, Paul. 2003. *The Liberation of the Laity: In Search of an Accountable Church.* New York: Continuum.

Lakeland, Paul. 2009. *Church: Living Communion.* Collegeville, MN: Liturgical Press.

Lane, Dermot. 2010. 'First Thoughts on the Murphy Report' in *The Furrow*, January 2010, 9-14.

Littleton, John, & Maher, Eamon, (eds). 2009. *What Being Catholic Means to Me.* Dublin: Columba Press.

Littleton, John. & Maher, Eamon, (eds). 2010. *The Dublin/Murphy Report: A Watershed for Irish Catholicism?* Dublin Columba Press.

McBrien, Richard P. 1994. *Catholicism* (New Edition). San Francisco: HarperSanFrancisco.

McCarthy, Pádraig. 2010. 'The Murphy Report: a personal assessment' in *The Furrow*, Vol 61, No 2, February 2010, pp 71-81.

McDonagh, Enda. 2010a. 'The Murphy and Ryan Reports: Between Evangelising and Priesthood' in *The Dublin/Murphy Report: A Watershed for Irish Catholicism?* (Littleton & Maher eds). Dublin: The Columba Press.

McDonagh, Enda. 2010. 'A Crucified People' in *The Furrow*, January 2010, 15-20.

McGahern, John. 2009. *Love of the World: Essays.* London: Faber & Faber.

McGee, H., Garaven, R., de Barra, M., Byrne, J. and Conroy, R. (2002). *The SAVI Report: Sexual Abuse and Violence in Ireland.* Dublin: The Liffey Press.

Maloney, Oliver. 2010. *The Furrow,* January 2010.

Mann, Elizabeth. 1999. 'Supervising in religious settings' in *Counselling Supervision in Context* (Carroll, Michael & Holloway, Elizabeth eds). London: SAGE.

Martin, James. 2007. 'How Could it Happen? An Analysis of the Catholic Sexual Abuse Scandal' in *Predatory Priests, Silenced Victims* (Frawley-O'Dea & Goldner eds). Mahwah, NJ: The Analytic Press.

May, Rollo. 1989. *The Art of Counselling,* Rev. Ed. New York: Gardner Press.

Marler, Penny Long & Hadaway, C Kirk. 2002. '"Being Religious" or "Being Spiritual" in America: A Zero-Sum Proporision?' in *Journal for the Scientific Study of Religion* 41:2 (2002), 289-300.

Merry, Johanna. 2010. 'Beyond the Shock Cycle.' in *The Furrow*, January 2010, pp 21-26.

Murphy, Jeffrie G. 2005. 'Forgiveness, Self-Respect, and the Value of Resentment' in *Handbook of Forgiveness* (Worthington, Everett L. ed). New York: Routledge.

Murphy, Mr Justice Francis D. 2005. *The Ferns Report.* Dublin: The Stationery Office.

Murphy, Seamus. 2010. 'No cheap grace: reforming the Irish church' in *Studies,* Vol 99, No 395. p 315).

Myers, David G. 2010. *Social Psychology.* (International Ed) New York: McGraw-Hill.

National Review Board, US Conference of Catholic Bishops. 2004. 'The Causes and Context of the Clergy Sexual Abuse of Minors Crisis' in *Origins,* Vol 33: No 39. pp 653-688. 11/03/2004.

Nichols, Michael P. 1991. *No Place to Hide: Facing Shame So We Can Find Self-Respect.* New York: Simon & Schuster.

Oakley, Lisa & Kathryn Kinmond. 2007. *Spiritual Abuse: raising awareness of a little-Understood form of abuse. Thresholds,* Summer 2007. pp 9-11.

O'Brien, Breda. 2010. 'Communicating the Good News and the Bad' in *The Dublin/Murphy Report: A Watershed for Irish Catholicism?* (Littleton & Maher eds). Dublin: Columba Press.

O'Gorman, Colm 2009. 'I Loved my Church Once' in *What Being Catholic Means to Me.* (Littleton, John & Maher Eamon eds) Dublin: Columba Press.

O'Gorman, Colm. 2009. *Beyond Belief: Abused by his priest, betrayed by his church, the story of the boy who sued the pope*. London: Hodder & Stoughton.
O'Neill, Onora. 2002. *A Question of Trust: The BBC Reith Lectures 2002*. Cambridge: Cambridge University Press.
O'Sullivan Garry. 2010. 'Quo Vadis? The Road to Rome' in *The Dublin/Murphy Report: A Watershed for Irish Catholicism?* (Littleton, John & Maher, Eamon eds) Dublin: The Columba Press.
Pope, Stephen J (ed). 2004. *Common Calling: The Laity & Governance of the Catholic Church*. Washington, DC: Georgetown University Press.
Pope, Stephen J. 2004. 'The Emerging Role of the Catholic Laity: Lessons from Voice of the Faithful' in *Common Calling: The Laity & Governance of the Catholic Church* (Pope, Stephen J. ed). Washington DC: Georgetown University Press.
Post, James E. 2006. 'Reflections on Ethics, Organizations and Church Culture' in *Church Ethics and Its Organizational Context* (Bartunek, Hinsdale & Keenan eds). Lanham, MD: Rowman & Littlefield.
Prendergast, Ned. 2010. 'In Brokenness We Awaken – a personal reflection after the Murphy Report' in *The Furrow*, April 2010. pp 199-206.
Pressman Donaldson, Stephanie & Pressman, Robert M. 1994. *Narcisstic Family: Diagnosis and Treatment*. San Francisco: Jossey-Bass.
Quinn, David. 2010. 'The Irish Media and the Murphy Report' in *Studies*, Vol 99, No 395 2010, pp 333-339.
Robertson, Geoffrey. 2010. *The Case of the Pope*. London: Penguin Books
Robinson, Bishop Geoffrey. 2007. *Confronting Power and Sex in the Catholic Church*. Dublin: Columba Press.
Robinson, Bryan E. 1998. *Chained to the Desk: A Guide for Workaholics, Their Partners and Children and the Clinicians Who Treat Them*. New York: New York University Press.
Rolheiser, Ronald. 1997. *The Holy Longing*. New York: Doubleday.
Rose, Jessica. 2009. *Church on Trial*. London: Darton, Longman & Todd.
Rossetti, Stephen J. 1996. *A Tragic Grace: The Catholic Church and Child Sexual Abuse*. Collegeville, MN: The Liturgical Press.
Rowe, D. 1991. *The Courage to Live*. London: HarperCollins.
Ruddy, Christopher. 2007. 'Ecclesiological Issues Behind the Sexual Abuse Crisis' in *Origins*, Vol 37, No 8, 5/07/2007. pp 119-126.
Ruth, Sean. 2006. *Leadership and Liberation: A Psychological Approach*. London: Routledge.
Ruth, Sean. 2010. 'Responding to Abuse: Culture, Leadership and Change' in *The Dublin/Murphy Report: A Watershed for Irish Catholicism?* (Littleton & Maher eds). Dublin: Columba Press.
Schaef, Anne Wilson & Diane Fassel. 1990. *The Addictive Organization*. San Francisco: HarperSanFrancisco.
Senge, Peter., Roberts, Charlotte., Ross, Richard B., Smith, Bryan J., Kleiner. 1994. *The Fifth Discipline Fieldbook: Strategies and Tools for Building a Learning Community*. New York: Currency/Doubleday.

Shea, John 1998. *Gospel Light: Jesus Stories for Spiritual Consciousness.* New York: A Crossroad Book.

Shields, Attracta. 1999. 'Child Sexual Abuse: A Systemic Approach' in *The Church and Child Sexual Abuse: Towards A Pastoral Response* (Conway, Eamonn *et al*, eds.). Dublin: The Columba Press.

Shupe, Anson. 2007. *Spoils of the Kingdom: Clergy Misconduct and Religious Community.* Urbana & Chicago: University of Illinois Press.

Shupe, Anson. 2008. Rogue Clerics: *The Social Problem of Clergy Deviance.* New Brunswick: Transaction Publishers.

Sipe, Richard A. W. 2003. *Celibacy in Crisis: A Secret World Revisited.* New York: Brunner-Routledge.

Sipe, Richard A. W. 2007. 'Introduction' in *Spoils of the Kingdom: Clergy Misconduct and Religious Community* (Shupe, Anson). Urbana & Chicago: University of Illinois Press.

Sontag, Susan. 2003. *Regarding the Pain of Others.* London: Penguin.

Sperry, Len. 2003. *Sex, Priestly Ministry and the Church.* Collegeville, MN: The Liturgical Press.

Spy, Terry 2004. 'Christianity, therapy and forgiveness' in *Forgiveness and the Healing Process: A Central Therapeutic Concern.* Hove, East Sussex: Brunner-Routledge.

Staub, Ervin. 2005. 'Constructive Rather Than Harmful Forgiveness, Reconciliation, and Ways to Promote Them After Genocide and Mass Killing' in *Handbook of Forgiveness.* (Worthington, Everett L. ed). New York: Routledge.

Sullivan, Francis A. 2000. 'The Papal Apology' in *America*, April 8, 2000. pp 17-22.

Tangney, June Price., Boone, Angela L., & Ronda Dearing. 2005. 'Forgiving the Self: Conceptual Issues and Empirical Findings' in *Handbook of Forgiveness* (Worthington, Everett L. ed). New York: Routledge.

Taylor, Charles. 2007. *A Secular Age.*

Templeton, Janice L. & Eccles, Jacquelynne S. 2006. 'The Relation Between Spiritual Development and Identity Porcesses' in *The Handbook of Spiritual Development in Childhood and Adolescence* (Roehlkepartain Eugence C. *et al*, eds). Thousand Oaks: Sage Publications.

Travers, Vincent. 2010. 'Cherishing and Protecting Our Children' in *Religious Life Review*, April 2010.

Weakland, Rembert G. 2002. 'Apology' in *Origins*, Vol 32, No 5, 2002.

Weakland, Rembert G. 2009. *A Pilgrim in a Pilgrim Church: Memoirs of a Catholic Archbishop.* Grand Rapids, Michigan: Wm. B. Eerdmans Publishing Co.

Weaver-Laport. 1993. 'Jansenism' in *The New Dictionary of Catholic Spirituality* (Downey, Michael, ed). Collegeville, MN: Michael Glazier.

Wehr, Demaris, S. 2000. 'Spiritual Abuse: When good people do bad things' in *The Psychology of Mature Spirituality* (Polly Young-

Eisendrath & Melvin E. Miller eds). London: Routledge.
Wilson, George B. 2008. *Clericalism: The Death of Priesthood.* Collegeville, MN: The Liturgical Press.
Wilson-Schaef, Anne. & Fassel, Diane. 1988. *The Addictive Organization.* San Francisco: HarperSanFrancisco.
Winkler Daryold Corbiere. 2001. 'Forgiveness and Reconciliation: Lessons from Canada's First Nations' in *The Challenge of Forgiveness* (Meier, Augustine & VanKatwyk, Peter, eds). Ottawa: Novalis.
Worden, William. 2009. *Grief Counseling and Grief Therapy: A Handbook for the Mental Health Practitioner* (4th. Ed.). New York: Springer Publishing Co.
Worthington, Everett L. 2003. *Forgiving and Reconciling: Bridges to Healing and Hope.* Downers Grove, Ill: Intervarsity Press.
Zinnbauer, Brian J and Pargament, Kenneth. 1998. 'Spiritual Conversion: A Study of Religious Change Among College Students' in *Journal for the Scientific Study of Religion*, Vol 37, No 1, pp 161-180.

Websites
I recommend the following websites were documentation referred to in this book can readily be accesssed:
www.dublindiocese.ie
www.catholicbishops.ie
www.justice.ie
www.originsonline.com
www.usccb.org
www.vatican.va